ELIZABETH CH(

Tiny Delights

The Companion to the TV Series

FOOD PHOTOGRAPHY BY JOHN HAY

f

I would like to dedicate this book to my grandchildren:

Fiona and Jessica, Gabrielle and Tess, and Jai,
who no matter how grown-up they become will always
remain my very own tiny delights.

—— ELIZABETH CHONG

Publisher: Ron Brown

First published in 2002 by Forté Communications
PO Box 1, Hawthorn Victoria 3122 Australia
Reprinted 2006

Text ©Elizabeth Chong, 2002
Photography © Forté Communications, 2002
All rights reserved.

Food photography by John Hay
Scenic China photography by Ron Brown
Step-by-step photography by Valeriu Campan
Photograph of Martin Yan courtesy Yan Can Cook Inc.
(photograph by Rosa To)
Antiques provided by Orient Express, Melbourne
Food styling by James Tan and Caroline Velik
Design and editing by Borghesi & Adam Publisners
Printed in China by Everbest Printing Co Ltd

National Library of Australia Cataloguing-in-Publication Data
Chong, Elizabeth.
    Tiny Delights : the companion to the T.V. series.
    ISBN 0 9580978 0 1
    1. Cookery, Chinese. 2. Dim sum. I. Title.
641.5951

PREFACE

Elizabeth Chong and I share two things in life — a common heritage and our great passion for Chinese food.

Like me, Elizabeth was born in Guangzhou. She moved with her family to Australia. In my case, it was Canada. We are both Chinese imports to the West. It was our love for great Chinese cuisine that first brought us together. We realized then that we both have as our mission to promote the culture and cuisine of China in the West, and we both chose television as our medium of communication.

This is the seventh book Elizabeth has authored. It's a companion to her current TV series, and she features a unique aspect of Chinese cuisine, the dim sum or yum cha dishes that are so uniquely Cantonese. Always thinking outside the box, she has extended this theme by adding other regional 'tiny delights': the simple dishes of Beijing in the north, Shanghai in the east, and Sichuan province in the west. The result is a panoramic culinary roadmap of Chinese delectables.

In selecting and presenting these dishes, Elizabeth introduces to her readers a lot more than just great recipes. She also brings a wealth of knowledge about Chinese food and culture. Her passionate writing style amply demonstrates the love of her Cantonese heritage and the home-style dishes that she learned as a girl from her mother. In collecting and creating these recipes, Elizabeth is generously enabling cooks and lovers of food around the world to share the rich heritage of the Chinese people.

Elizabeth is often referred to as a 'living treasure' by her peers, and she recently celebrated the fortieth anniversary of her cooking school in Melbourne, Australia. As an admirer of her talent and dedication, her hard work and total commitment to her calling forever inspire me.

Enjoy this book, use and experiment with the recipes you will find here, because this truly is a collection of 'tiny delights'.

Martin Yan
HOST, YAN CAN COOK

CONTENTS

CHINA

Beijing

Shanghai
Hangzhou

Chengdu

Guangzhou

Hong Kong

Following page:

Elizabeth at the Dragon Well
tea plantation, Hangzhou.

INTRODUCTION

I have always had a love affair with my native cuisine. Simple family meals bring back precious memories of my mother's fragrant home soups, almost impossible to rival: her everyday dishes, plain in presentation, earthy, savoury, deceptively simple; her dumplings, delicate and delicious with just the right amount of dried shrimps and seasoning. And for the grand occasions: Murray cod, steamed to perfection (my father's favorite); succulently rich abalone; wind-dried meats teamed with jade-green mustard cabbage — an endless succession of Chinese haute cuisine to build a dream upon.

Over four decades now, I have shared this deep love and pride in Chinese food. Some 36000 students have passed through my kitchen door and through the media of television, radio and print many more have been encouraged to explore the simplicity and complexities of one of the world's greatest cuisines.

The Chinese have always cooked 'big'. The rice pot was filled to the brim, the soup pot was huge and as the extended family gathered together at the end of the day, it was with thanksgiving around the family table. Sadly, the extended family living together under one roof is almost legendary now, even in China.

Traditionally, the Chinese place an assortment of dishes in the centre of the table from which each diner takes small amounts of each. This is quite different to the Western custom of serving meals on individual plates. Although the Chinese do not normally think in terms of 'serves', I have included the approximate number for each recipe, as a rough guide for those less accustomed to serving meals the Chinese way.

The pleasure of eating small amounts of one dish surely originated in China. Peking Duck is the perfect tiny delight of crisp chestnut-brown skin, a julienne of cucumber and spring onion encased in a wafer pancake, and is designed to be only two exquisite mouthfuls. Even family-sized dishes are designed so each member eats only a small portion of each dish, and the unique Cantonese institution of dim sum or yum cha is the epitome of tiny delights. *Tiny Delights*, with its collection of delectable small Chinese dishes, meets the needs of singles, couples and small families. If, by happy chance, one becomes two, then three or four, simple multiplication is all that is necessary.

My television series *Tiny Delights* and this accompanying book are milestones in a long and satisfying career. I have always seen myself as a bridge between two worlds, and bringing them together through food has been my joy, my passion, and my challenge. I am not sure if I believe in destiny, but somehow my life has followed a natural, almost inevitable way, and this last journey took me back to my homeland, the place of my birth, so I could portray to you the real story of China's tiny delights.

Elizabeth Chong

Chinese legend tells the story of Emperor Shen Nung, who discovered the joys of tea-drinking some 5000 years ago while relaxing under the shade of a camellia tree. As he fell into a light sleep, a gentle breeze blew a few young, tipped leaves from the tree into his cup of boiled water. He woke and took a few sips, not noticing the leaves at first, and was astonished at the delicate fragrance and flavor. Henceforth by royal decree, his boiled water was to always have the green tips of the camellia plant.

Well, it's a nice story and who today would dispute it? But there is evidence that tea was drunk in China as early as AD300. The leaves were gathered from the wild and the brew was drunk by poor folk more for medicinal than gustatory purposes. It was often prescribed for digestive and nervous conditions, and is today appreciated for the same qualities.

By AD600, tea was also drunk for pleasure, and the cultivation of the *camellia sinensis* plant had begun. Less than 200 years later, the drinking of tea had become something of a cult among the literate and the upper class of China. The renowned scholar, Lu Yu, who wrote his famous three-volume tea classic, *The Book of Tea,* covered everything to do with tea from its proper cultivation to the brewing and its contemplative enjoyment. After that, tea-drinking and the appreciation of it was a prerequisite for anyone aspiring to some recognized high level of society, and was indeed a form of snobbery.

As cultivation ensured a more plentiful supply, tea became the beverage of choice for everyone, rich and poor. Britain wanted China's tea and was willing to fight for it, and fight they did! Their weapon was opium, and finally China was forced to cede the territory of Hong Kong to the British. If it were not for tea, Hong Kong would probably have become a fishing port and Kowloon an agricultural community, for Hong Kong was created expressly for carrying on the tea trade.

Facing page:

Tea house overlooking West Lake, Hangzhou.

Today, the English still love a good, strong cup of tea 'to get them through trouble', the Americans drink iced tea with lemon, the Irish like theirs powerfully strong and black, while in Morocco they love it with mint and sugar and in Australia 'billy tea' is immortalized in the national song, 'Waltzing Matilda'. The Chinese drink their tea black without milk or sugar and drink more than anyone else. They set no special time to drink it — any time is the right time.

The varieties of Chinese tea are almost endless, with each region producing and blending its own speciality. Differing geographic conditions and climates account for the multitude of varieties in the same way as they affect grape-growing for wine. One species of tea is grown in such high, inaccessible places that monkeys are trained to pick the leaves.

Chinese teas are graded into green (unfermented) and black (fermented) tea. A semi-fermented tea is called Oolong tea. The smallest leaves are considered to be the best, because they have not yet developed tannic acid which gives a bitter taste. After the processing and brewing of the leaves, special fragrances can be added such as jasmine, chrysanthemum and lychee flowers.

Tea houses and salons welcome lovers of tea and serve delicate morsels created specially to accompany tea. This unique custom is called 'yum cha' (to drink tea) or 'dim sum' (to touch the heart), during which the teapot is replenished constantly. It is said that one can indulge in as many pastries as liked, without ill effects, if tea accompanies the food.

No cup of tea is better than its leaves, and there are a few rules to follow to get the best result: Always rinse out your teapot or cup with hot water first before adding the tea leaves. Some like their water at a rolling boil, while others say the water should be 'just beginning to dance' (almost at a full boil) before being poured over the leaves.

The Chinese say tea helps to reduce carcinogens in the body, is a tonic for the blood vessels, even helps to fight tooth decay, and when it is drunk wisely, ritually and regularly, promotes a state of mind that reduces stress and preserves youth. Anyone for a cup of tea?

Facing page:
A teapot vendor's wares
in Old Shanghai.

11

EQUIPMENT AND TECHNIQUES

MEASUREMENT NOTES

All cup measures are based on a standard metric cup (250 ml). To convert to fluid ounces, see the conversion chart below. All spoon measures are level. All oven temperatures are given in Celsius (°C) followed by the Fahrenheit equivalent (°F).

The recipes provide both metric measurements and their imperial equivalents. In many instances, only an approximate conversion is given and that is quite adequate; if a precise conversion is required for a given recipe, it is provided. The following chart is a useful additional reference.

CHANGE	TO	MULTIPLY BY
centimetres	inches	0.3937
grams	ounces	0.0353
grams	pounds	0.002205
kilograms	pounds	2.2046
millimetres	inches	0.0394
millilitres	fluid ounces	0.0333

If you were to take a tour of several Chinese kitchens, you would be struck by the similarities. The kitchens of star restaurants and top international hotels throughout Asia are set out with the same kitchen equipment and utensils as the modest little wayside cafes. Certainly, there would be modern flooring and sparkling tiles on the walls, but you would see little evidence of expensive, electrical gadgetry, food processors and machinery, no matter how fancy the establishments. Instead, you would see the same wooden chopping boards (sawn-off sections of a native tree), an assemblage of the traditional tempered steel woks and exactly the same implements and utensils. The most elaborate banquet is prepared with the simple tools used in the home by the housewife. Restaurant chefs use bigger and heavier choppers and woks, but there the difference ends.

Chinese cooking does not always require the complicated, involved preparation most people imagine, although at times it certainly can. The famous Emperor's Banquet, still available today (if you have time to spend four days eating it and the pocket to go with it!) involves preparation on a scale unheard of in the Western world. Yet the fact remains even a banquet like this is prepared with no more than a few simple tools.

For everyday meals, it is the same as for any other cuisine: the preparation and cooking of food is a matter of commonsense, the right instruction, a little imagination and a little love. So put away all your fancy kitchen gadgets and elaborate electric machines, and use the simple equipment and preparation methods explained on the following pages.

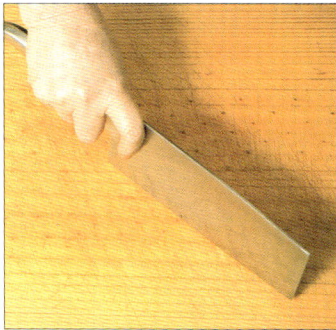

1

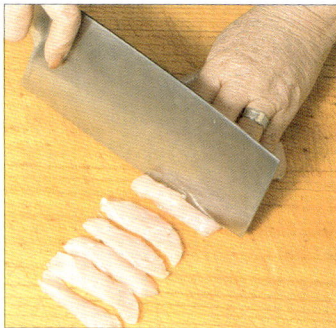

2

3

USING YOUR CHINESE CHOPPER

Your best friend in a Chinese kitchen. Life for one day without the chopper is a day fraught with frustration and despair. It may look fearsomely wicked, but overcome your initial reluctance and with a little practice you will become so attached to it, you will forget your other kitchen knives. Ideally, you should have two choppers: one for fine slicing and one for chopping through bones; however, an all-purpose Number 3 will suffice the average cook. It should be kept sharp in the same manner as other knives.

How to hold your chopper: With your right hand (or your left, if you are left-handed), firmly grasp the handle close to the blade (thumb outstretched) with your index finger stretched along the other side of the blade for balance (see 1, left).

Although it is called a chopper, it does more fine slicing than anything else. For slicing, never lift the blade above the knuckles of your other hand. Even when chopping through bones, the blade is not lifted very high. The way food is cut will greatly determine how it will taste.

Slicing: Hold the item firmly on the chopping board with your left hand (or your right, if you are right-handed). The fingers should be curved and tucked under, the knuckles resting lightly against the back of the blade. Using the joints of the fingers as a guide, slice straight through with one forward movement, with the blade slightly turned outwards, then move the fingers back slightly and repeat the movement. Meat is always sliced across the grain and slices are approximately 4 cm (1½ inch) long and 3 mm (⅛ inch) thick (2, left).

Diagonal slicing: This technique is the same as the above, but hold your chopper at an angle of 45 degrees away from you. Slice right through at this angle. Diagonal slicing is mainly used for vegetables (3, left).

14

Chopping: Chop straight through poultry bones (cooked or uncooked) with a straight sharp motion. Use the end of the blade closest to the handle as you can apply more weight at this point. Do not raise the chopper too high.

Crushing: Ginger, garlic, and spring onions are sometimes crushed to release full flavors. Place them on the chopping board and hit with the flat surface of the chopper. Don't be too enthusiastic about hitting, or the food will be pulped!

Cubing or dicing: Cut the meat or vegetables into strips, stack, then cut across into even cubes or dice. Cubing is larger than dicing. Cubing strips would generally be approximately 2 cm (¾ inch) wide and dicing strips approximately 5 mm–1 cm (¼ inch–½ inch) wide (4, right).

Mincing: Dice the meat then crush with the chopper. Chop downwards with short, quick strokes until the pieces are very fine. Scoop up the meat with the chopper, pile into the centre of the board, and repeat until minced (5, right).

Shredding: First slice the meat or vegetable (see *Slicing*). Stack and cut into fine julienne strips. The length should never exceed 5 cm (2 inches). (6, right).

Scooping: Place the chopper blade under the prepared ingredients and with your other hand carefully push the food onto the wide blade. The food can then be transferred to a plate or taken straight to the wok. It saves a lot of time!

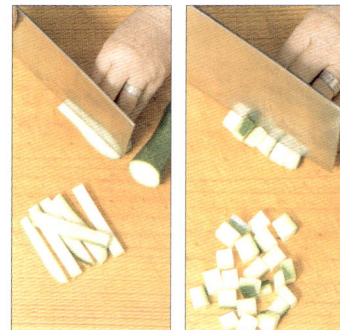

4

5

6

15

7

8

9

Roll cutting: For vegetables that are round in shape, for example, zucchinis, carrots, and asparagus, angle your chopper at 45 degrees and cut through as in diagonal slicing, then roll the vegetable towards you one quarter of a turn and diagonally slice again. Repeat (7, left).

Scoring: This is often used to prepare fish, squid and kidneys for appearance, for tenderizing and for allowing greater penetration of flavors and heat. Criss-cross cutting is generally quite shallow with the slicing angled (8, left).

Wedge cutting: Ingredients should be approximately 2.5 cm (1 inch) in width across. Make the first slice with the chopper at a 45-degree angle then angle the chopper the opposite way. This makes triangular shaped pieces (9, left).

DE-VEINING PRAWNS

Slice along the back of the shelled prawn (being careful not to cut through). Remove the black thread, then wash under running water and gently pat dry.

SKINNING A FISH

Lay the fillet of fish skin-side down on the chopping board. Cut through the flesh to the skin with the chopper. Keep a firm hold of the skin with the fingers and remove the flesh with the chopper, separating from the skin.

THE WOK

The wok is a miraculous pan, probably the most versatile cooking vessel ever created. It has no need for design changes after centuries of millions of satisfied users. Many attempts to modernize it have created unnecessary fuss and expense which, at the same time, fall far short in function from the traditional rolled tempered steel wok, which responds well to changes of heat and conducts it quickly and evenly.

The curved, shallow bowl shape of the wok makes it excellent for stir-frying, as the sloping sides facilitate the tossing and turning of ingredients essential for quick cooking. Deep-frying is efficient also; the wide area allows for great freedom in moving the foods in the oil and because of the rounded bottom much less oil is needed. Whether it be shallow-frying (such as for sausages, steaks, braising meats), steaming or boiling, the wok will happily cook anything from an egg to a chicken.

The rounded bottom has caused concern for some stoves especially electric plates, and an iron ring frame can be used to support the wok more steadily, but better still is a wok with a very slightly flattened bottom which entirely eliminates any wobbling. Be sure the flattened area at the base is only a few inches across and the inside of the wok is still smoothly rounded. Woks featuring a wide flat bottom are really glorified English frying pans and will not perform efficiently for Chinese cooking. You should select woks made only by the Chinese for the Chinese.

To season your wok, first wash it in warm soapy water and dry well. Place on a very low heat and rub the surface with a cloth pad impregnated with peanut oil. Continue to rub while heating until the pad comes out clean. Wash and dry again, rubbing a little oil on the surface each time before putting it away. It is a good idea to soak the wok in warm soapy water immediately after use if you cannot wash it immediately; any food burnt on to the surface will then lift off easily with a cloth. Steel wool and mild soap will not harm your wok; just make sure it is dry before putting it away. If your new wok has a coating of varnish on it, then three-quarters fill it with water with two tablespoons of bicarbonate of soda. Boil vigorously for 15 minutes, scrubbing with a sink brush to help lift off the varnish, then wash in the normal way and season. Your wok will darken with age and use. Don't worry! A black wok is the proud hallmark of a good cook.

DEEP-FRYING WITH YOUR WOK

You cannot be too cavalier when deep-frying in your wok, and caution is needed. The wok should never be more than one-third filled with oil, and must be stable. Don't let it rock while you are cooking, and never leave it unattended. Avoid over-heating the oil; once it just begins to smoke it is hot enough. Slide the food into the wok as this will minimize splashing.

STIR-FRYING WITH YOUR WOK

This is the fastest way to cook ingredients that have been cut into bite-size portions. It often takes less than a minute, and seldom more than three. A small amount of oil is heated in the wok and the food is constantly stirred and tossed around until done. Sometimes (in the case of vegetables) a small amount of liquid is added after the initial frying. The wok is covered with a lid enabling the food to be cooked in its own juice.

In stir-frying, the heat of the wok is critical. This is what the Chinese call correct 'wok hay'. It is a good cook who really understands 'wok hay'. You must learn to toss and turn the foods quickly, so they will not burn, but will acquire a light glazing of hot oil that ensures the flavors and juices are locked inside the ingredients. You have to ensure even after a small amount of liquid is added and the lid placed on that the heat is still at maximum point. There is a Western tendency to turn the heat down too low and 'stew' the meat and vegetables.

USING YOUR STEAMER

The food is placed in a dish or plate suspended above water (usually in a wok), and steamed until done. The dish can also be placed in a special bamboo steamer. Fish and minced dishes cook particularly well this way; flavors are added to the food before steaming and the dish is brought from the steamer straight to the table. It is a method which brings out purity of taste, and is recommended for the health conscious.

When using a bamboo steamer, the food is put on a dish inside the steamer basket with the bamboo lid on top, then placed over boiling water in the wok to steam. Bamboo minimizes condensation as it is porous, and it is especially suitable for steaming buns and dim sims. The steamers come in layers, and can be stacked one on top of the other, with one lid. When you have purchased a new steamer, rub some cooking oil between the bamboo slats to help prevent sticking.

Apart from the many steamed dishes in the Chinese cuisine, such as fish and minced meats, steaming is an excellent way of re-heating your food. Steamers should be at least 5 cm (2 inches) smaller in diameter than your wok.

If you do not have a wok or a steamer, and you are looking for an alternative way of steaming food, try the following method: place a wire rack in an electric fry pan. Put about 2.5 cm (one inch) of boiling water in the bottom of the pan and place your plate of food on the rack. Just be sure there is not so much water that it will touch the food while it is cooking. Cover the pan with the lid and with the vent open. Maintain a gentle steady steam (usually about 150°C [300°F] keeps the water simmering). If you are steaming fish be sure the temperature is not so high that it creates too vigorous a steam. The delicate flesh could disintegrate from too much and too long a steaming.

20

CHOPSTICKS

Bamboo or wooden chopsticks can be used to prepare food. They are truly an extension of your own hand; they stir, beat, whisk, pick up, turn over and separate foods in the wok. Chopsticks for the table come in bamboo, lacquered wood, bone, ivory and in lavish jade, agate, gold and silver.

CHOPPING BOARD

The traditional Chinese chopping board is a level cross-section of a tree trunk. This board is still favored by the Chinese, particularly in restaurants, as a large one is so heavy it will not move during chopping. It is also kinder to the blades of the chopper. Most modern homes, however, find it a little tedious to maintain and wash, as it should never be submerged in water. A sturdy wooden or polyurethene board is adequate. Never use a slippery-surfaced cutting board on which your food will slip and slide and which will also blunt your knife.

WOK SPATULA

The right companion for your wok is the Chinese spatula, literally called the 'wok shovel' by the Chinese. This is curved to fit exactly the sloping sides of the wok, and possesses surprising strength. It is inexpensive and a great joy to use. Spatulas made from iron or stainless steel are practical, but be sure to thoroughly dry them before putting away.

STRAINER OR SKIMMER

An essential accessory especially for lifting foods deep-fried in oil and for straining hot liquids. The long handle protects your hand from hot steam and burning oils. The new stainless steel strainers are perhaps not quite as decorative as the old-fashioned wire skimmers, but they are easy to clean.

Steamed Rice

Properly cooked rice using the absorption method is an absolute necessity to your Chinese cooking skills. It is very easy, and takes about five minutes' preparation and 40 minutes to cook. The method below is suitable for either long or short grain white rice. Always allow half a cup of uncooked rice for each person, remembering that rice doubles in volume when it is cocked.

Place the rice in a saucepan and wash in cold water. Swill it around until the water becomes cloudy and milky. Rinse, then add more water and repeat until the water is clear (I was taught to wash the rice seven times!). Now, cover the rice with water.

The water should rise to 1 cm (about half an inch) above the level of the rice. If, however, you are cooking only a small quantity (less than two cups of rice), just 5 mm (about quarter of an inch) of water above the level of the washed rice is enough. If you are cooking a large amount (say, six cups or more), then 2 cm (about three-quarters of an inch) of water to cover is all that is needed.

Cover the rice and water with a lid. To cook, bring the rice to a rapid boil over a high heat. When the water starts to bubble over, reduce the heat only enough to arrest it. Continue on medium heat until the water is absorbed. The rice should still be moist, with little 'craters', but there must not be any loose water in the pot before you reduce the heat to a low simmer. You may stir the rice just before turning down the heat.

Simmer for 15–20 minutes. Longer simmering will not harm the rice, but you will probably get a 'crust' on the bottom of the saucepan, and if you are cooking a very small amount of rice then you will end up with only a little to eat.

The fine layer of 'crust' is quite normal, especially if you are cooking a fairly large amount of rice, as the simmering can be extended to a longer period of time. This simmering period is the actual cooking process needed in order to cook each grain through to perfection.

The Chinese believe undercooked rice causes indigestion and gives rise to a number of other ailments.

The crust on the bottom of the saucepan is an indication that the rice has had the proper steaming time. It should be a very light golden color; if it is darker than this then you have not turned your heat low enough and you may have even burnt the rice.

No salt is added to Chinese steamed rice. The saucepan is tightly covered with a lid throughout the cooking time, locking in the steam. Because the water has been absorbed, the rice is steamed rather than boiled.

This absorption means that the amount of water used is exactly the right amount to cook the rice grains — no more, no less! When properly cooked, the grains should be tender inside and out without being 'mushy'. The grains are separate, yet have a certain stickiness (not to be confused with glugginess!). When rice has been washed after cooking (usually in a desperate attempt to separate grains), the flavor, vitamins and texture are washed out. To the Chinese, rice must have 'body' if it is to be at all satisfying.

On a sampan on the Pearl River,
heading for Guangzhou . . .

Won Ton Soup

Won tons are little dumplings filled with pork or prawns and are enjoyed in a bowl of clear chicken soup. 'Won' means cloud and 'ton' means swallow — since won ton wrappers are so light and fragile the experience is like swallowing clouds! Chinese poetic licence, but then why not?

60g/2oz fresh shelled prawns

60g/2oz minced pork

*4 Chinese dried shiitake
    mushrooms, soaked for 1
    hour, stalks removed then
    finely chopped*

*¼ cup water chestnuts,
    finely chopped*

*2 tbs bamboo shoots, drained
    and finely chopped*

*2 tsp har mai (dried shrimps),
    soaked 10–15 minutes in warm
    water then finely chopped*

½ tsp fresh ginger, finely minced

*½ cup spring onions,
    finely chopped*

1 tbs egg, lightly beaten

½ tsp corn flour

1 tsp salt

pinch pepper

*30 won ton wrappers,
    7.5cm/3in square*

4 cups chicken broth

2 slices fresh ginger (extra)

extra salt

*a few drops of light soy sauce and
    sesame oil (to taste)*

*serves 2–15
(as many or as few as you like!)*

PREPARATION

De-vein and wash the prawns, then mince with the chopper. To make the filling, mix the prawns in a bowl together with the pork, mushrooms, water chestnuts, bamboo shoots, har mai, ginger, corn flour, spring onions, egg, salt and pepper. (Reserve some of the green part of the spring onion for the garnish.)

There are many ways to fold won tons, but this is one of the easiest: Lay one won ton wrapper in a flat diamond shape on your preparation bench. Place one teaspoon of the filling towards the middle of the wrapper, just down from the centre (see the step-by-step photographs on the following page). Fold the wrapper over to form a triangle (the bottom layer should be slightly larger than the top), then twist the bottom right corner to meet the back of the left corner. Press to seal, using a little water if necessary. Continue until you have made them all.

TO COOK

Heat the pot of chicken broth, and add two slices of fresh ginger and salt to taste.

Bring a separate pot of water to the boil and drop in the won tons. Keep the water on the boil until the won tons float (about two minutes), then remove them with a skimmer or slotted spoon and place in individual soup bowls. For a light meal, place six or so in a bowl; for a full meal, the sky is the limit!

Spoon the boiling chicken broth over the won tons. Add a sprinkle of light soy sauce and sesame oil, and garnish with chopped spring onions.

1 Lay the won ton wrapper in a diamond shape on the bench. Place one teaspoon of the filling towards the middle of the wrapper, just down from the centre.

2 Fold the wrapper over to form a triangle. (The bottom layer should be slightly larger than the top.)

3 Twist the bottom right corner to meet the back of the left corner.

4 Press to seal, using a little water if necessary.

1

2

3

4

Facing page:

Elizabeth at the free market in Guangzhou.

Five Willows Prawns

This is a beautiful dish for lovers of prawns. The sauce is piquant, and with its pretty colors is a garnish in itself.

*8 king or banana prawns
(fresh or frozen), with shells
and heads removed,
and tails intact.*
a dash of salt and pepper
3 tbs peanut oil
*1 stalk spring onion, cut into
5cm/2in pieces and lightly
slapped with the broad part of
the chopper (use mainly the
white part of the onion)*
1 slice fresh ginger
*1 tbs each of carrot, cucumber,
capsicum and Chinese
mixed pickles, cut into
julienne strips*

for the sauce:
mix together
2 tbs vinegar
1 tbs sugar
2 tbs water
2 tsp hoi sin sauce
*a few drops tabasco sauce
(optional)*
1 tsp corn flour

serves 2

PREPARATION

Prepare the sauce by mixing all the sauce ingredients together in a bowl or jug. Put to one side.

De-vein and wash the prawns. Cut them into bite-sized chunks and sprinkle with salt and pepper.

TO COOK

Heat the peanut oil in a pre-heated wok, swirling around gently until just smoking. Add the spring onions and ginger to sizzle for two minutes, then remove and discard.

Add the prawns to the wok and stir-fry in moderately hot oil for about 30 seconds. Remove and place on a plate.

Add the vegetable strips to the wok (there should be about one tablespoon of oil remaining in the wok). Stir-fry the strips over gentle heat for two minutes.

Stir in the prepared sauce until it thickens and bubbles, then spoon the sauce and vegetables over the prawns.

Provincial Chicken

This dish is my favorite 'homestyle' chicken dish. It is one of the first dishes I cook when I have been away from home for a while, perhaps because it brings back memories of my childhood days. Whatever the reason, my own children have inherited the same devotion to this old family favorite! It is also a good dish for those watching their diet and for busy people who do not have much time to spend on food preparation. It takes about five minutes to put together, is low in fat, and there is practically no washing-up!

250g/8 oz chicken pieces, or chicken wings only
4 Chinese dried shiitake mushrooms, soaked for 30 minutes, stalks removed, then sliced into julienne strips
2 tsp doong choi (Chinese preserved vegetable)
1 tsp fresh ginger, shredded
2 tsp light soy sauce
1 tsp fish sauce
good pinch of salt
1 tsp corn flour dissolved in 1 tbs cold water

to serve:
steamed rice
assorted green vegetables

serves 2

PREPARATION

Wash the chicken pieces and chop into largish bite-sized pieces. If you include the bones, it will be a tastier dish.

Mix everything together and place in a small dish similar to a pie dish or shallow soup bowl.

TO COOK

Place the dish on a steaming rack in the wok over boiling water and steam for 15 minutes. Remove and serve straight from the dish. Serve with freshly steamed rice and some green vegetables.

Pearl Balls

Glutinous rice has a special place in ancient festival foods in China, such as the 'sticky rice parcels' wrapped in lotus leaves on the fifth day of the fifth month to celebrate the Lantern Festival.

It is also enjoyed in a special rice pudding at Chinese New Year celebrations. Glutinous rice has been traced back to archaeological excavations of the early Han period (206 BC–AD 220). This is a dish sometimes included in the yum cha range.

6 tbs glutinous rice
12oz/375g minced pork
½ egg, lightly beaten
1 tsp light soy sauce
½ tsp salt
few drops fish sauce
2 tsp corn flour
1 tsp ginger, minced
6 dried Chinese shiitake
   mushrooms, soaked for 30
   minutes, stalks removed, then
   finely chopped
6 water chestnuts,
   finely chopped
¼ cup fresh coriander or spring
   onions, chopped

for the garnish:
extra coriander, fresh
some chutney or plum sauce

serves 2–3

PREPARATION

Soak the rice in 1¼ cups of cold water for a minimum of two hours, then strain.

Place the pork, egg, soy sauce, salt, fish sauce, corn flour and ginger in a bowl and combine well. Add the mushrooms, water chestnuts and the coriander and mix through.

Scoop up a tablespoon of the meat mixture into the palm of your hand and shape into a ball (about the size of a ping pong ball). It is a good idea to moisten your hands with a little cold water from time to time. Roll the pork balls into the rice grains, pressing them in quite firmly as you roll.

TO COOK

Lightly grease a steaming basket or a plate. Add the pearl balls and steam over boiling water for 20 minutes. Keep the water at a good rolling boil and replenish if necessary. Garnish with the fresh coriander. Serve as a main meat dish with plum sauce or with your own chutney.

白發粉麵廠

A bustling, open-air street market.
'In China, shopping for food is a daily task
and freshness is almost an obsession . . .'

Cantonese Fried Rice

This can be a really complete meal for a single — or double! A good balance is achieved from the combination of grains (rice), vegetables (bean sprouts and spring onions), and protein (pork, eggs). Fried rice is best made from cold rice.

2 cups cold cooked rice
   (brown or white)
1/2 tsp salt
125g/4oz char shui
   (Chinese roast pork)
100g fresh prawn meat
2 tbs peanut oil
3 eggs, lightly beaten with
   a little salt
1/2 cup fresh bean sprouts, or
   finely chopped celery
2 tbs red capsicum, diced
1 stalk spring onion, chopped
2 tsp light soy sauce
few drops of sesame oil

serves 2

PREPARATION

Work the salt through the rice with the fingers, breaking up any hard lumps.

Dice the char shui and prawn meat into small cubes.

TO COOK

Heat the wok, add the oil and heat until it is just smoking. Stir-fry the prawns for a few seconds.

Pour the beaten eggs into the centre of the wok, and allow to cook until softly set.

Add the rice, working it well into the heat of the wok, and mixing thoroughly with the eggs and prawn meat. This takes about two minutes.

Add the char shui, bean sprouts (or celery), capsicum and spring onions and toss through the rice until the sprouts are softened just a little. Sprinkle in the soy sauce and sesame oil, toss through evenly, and serve.

Note: You may substitute bacon or ham for the char shui if you wish. If you do, be sure to stir-fry the bacon or ham together with the prawns before adding the other ingredients.

Hainan Chicken Rice

This dish comes from an island off the south coast of China, but I have enjoyed it the most in a Singapore cafe where it is a popular dish with the locals. It is a complete meal for one or two!

1 small whole chicken
1 tsp salt
2 cups rice
¼ cup chicken fat removed from
    the chicken (or make-up
    quantity with peanut oil)
3 cloves garlic, slapped lightly
    with the broad side of the
    chopper to remove outer skin
    (be careful not to break the
    garlic flesh)
1 slice fresh ginger
    5mm/¼in thick
2 cups clear chicken soup

for the chilli dip:
1 tsp chilli sauce
1 tsp ginger, finely minced
½ tsp garlic, minced
squeeze of lemon or lime juice

for the ginger dip:
2 tsp ginger, finely shredded
2 tsp spring onion, shredded
1 tbs peanut oil
dash of salt and pepper

for the soy dip:
1 tbs soy sauce
few drops of sesame oil

serves 2

PREPARATION

Mix the ingredients for each dip together in three separate bowls. Put to one side.

Wash the chicken under cold running water and pat dry. Rub all over with a little salt and let stand for 15 minutes. Place the chicken in a pot with enough cold water to cover and bring to the boil. Once boiling, maintain on a gentle boil for 10–12 minutes, or until the chicken is cooked. Turn off the heat and allow the chicken to cool in the stock, then remove to a plate. Keep the stock for cooking the rice, then wash the rice.

Chop the chicken into small pieces, Chinese-fashion, and arrange on a plate. Slice the chicken fat into shreds and assemble on another plate with the garlic, ginger and rice.

TO COOK

In a pre-heated wok, heat the chicken fat until it has melted. Remove any unmelted remains. Add the rice; turn up the heat and stir-fry on high for two minutes. Remove the rice and place in a saucepan, ready for cooking. Add the garlic and ginger to the wok and sauté for one or two minutes (be careful not to burn the garlic). Remove and put to one side.

Pour enough of the reserved stock into the saucepan so it covers the rice and rises about one centimetre (roughly half an inch) above it. Add the garlic and ginger, and cook the rice (see Steamed Rice, page 22). Serve with the chopped chicken (drizzled with soy sauce if you wish), dips, fresh greens (lettuce, cabbage, etc.) and bowls of clear chicken soup.

Sung Choi Bao

The Chinese have surprising ways of serving lettuce. Lettuce dropped in a clear chicken broth makes a delicately beautiful soup, or braised lettuce tossed for a few minutes in a garlic-flavored oil is a superb base for exotic dishes like stuffed mushrooms and abalone in oyster sauce.

The following recipe uses crunchy lettuce leaves as wrappings or pancakes. The surprise is in the filling. Beef or chicken are equally popular fillings for these Sung Choi Bao, whilst quail, pigeon or roast duckling make them rather special.

4 lettuce leaves (iceberg) refreshed in cold water, dried and left to crisp in the refrigerator

1 tsp corn flour dissolved in 2 tbs cold water (thickening)

2 tbs peanut oil

for the filling:
125g/4oz minced pork (pork fillet can be used)
1 lup chiang (Chinese sausage) steamed for 10 minutes then diced
¼ cup water chestnuts, roughly chopped
1 tbs spring onions, chopped (use mainly the white part)

for the seasoning:
½ tsp salt
dash of pepper
1 tbs shaohsing wine (Chinese rice wine)
1 tsp light soy sauce
1 tsp oyster sauce

serves 2

PREPARATION

Mix together the filling ingredients in a bowl, ready for frying. Mix together the seasoning ingredients in a separate bowl.

TO COOK

Heat the peanut oil in the wok until it is just smoking, then stir-fry the filling mixture until the color changes (this will take about two minutes).

Add the seasoning, toss well, then stir in the corn flour thickening until boiling. Add a dash of water if needed.

Serve crisp lettuce leaves separately with the filling.

The meat is spooned into each leaf, and rolled up to make a little parcel. Eat with the fingers.

Easy Chicken Wings

This has become a popular family dish — partly because it is so economical! At the same time, the Chinese revere the wings above any other part of the chicken because of the silky texture.

I have cooked chicken wings by the hundreds for children's parties and they have always been a favorite. Yet I remember back in the 1960s people in Australia didn't really eat them. Around that time, my local supermarket tried to sell them, but no-one wanted them so they gave the lot to me! Things must have started to catch on, however, because a few weeks later I noticed they were no longer free and were selling very quickly . . .

1 kg chicken wings
2 tbs peanut oil
2 tbs light soy sauce
2 tbs shaohsing wine
   (Chinese rice wine)
2 tbs tomato sauce
2 tbs honey
2 cloves garlic, minced
1 tsp salt
½ tsp five-spice powder
2 tsp chilli sauce
   (or sambal oelek)

serves 2–4

PREPARATION

Wash the chicken wings, and remove the tips. Dry with paper towels.

Mix all the other ingredients together in a bowl to make the marinade. Add the wings and allow to stand for one hour.

TO COOK

Pre-heat the oven to 180°C (350°F).

Place the wings on an oven tray (a tray without sides gives the best results).

Roast in the centre of the oven for 45 minutes, then serve.

The fishing village at Lei Yue Mun, H.K.

'fish is a symbol of prosperity, abundance and good luck. At Lei Yue Mun, the fish are swimming – no – jumping fresh.'

Scallop Egg Rolls

This elegant dish can be prepared entirely beforehand and heated up for a few minutes before serving, making it perfect for entertaining.

2 eggs
250g/8oz fresh scallops
1 tsp ginger juice
   (use a garlic squeezer)
½ cup chives, finely chopped
   (use mainly the white part)
1 tbs peanut oil
2 nori sheets (15cm/6in in
   diameter)
2 tbs fish roe (or caviar)
few drops oyster sauce
   (optional)

serves 2–4

PREPARATION

Break the eggs and reserve two teaspoons of egg white. Lightly beat the remaining eggs together with half a teaspoon of salt and put to one side.

Wash and dry the scallops, then chop to a rough mince. Add the ginger juice, reserved egg white and chives and mix through.

TO COOK

Lightly oil a flat 15 cm (6 inch) frying pan. Pour in enough of the egg mixture to form a thin pancake. Cook over moderate heat until one side is dry, then flip over to the other side for about ten seconds. Remove from heat. Repeat to make a second pancake.

Generously spread the scallop mixture evenly over each egg pancake with a butter knife, right to the edges.

Lay one nori sheet circle over each pancake and gently press to seal. Roll up each pancake quite firmly like a Swiss roll, and place on a lightly oiled steaming plate. Steam over gentle heat for six or seven minutes.

Remove the rolls to a cutting board and cut each roll diagonally at 1 cm (½ inch) intervals. (They will look like little pinwheels.)

Arrange the rolls on a warm serving plate, dotted with the fish roe. Drizzle a little oyster sauce over the top if you wish.

Steamed Oysters
in Black Bean Sauce

I have not eaten this dish outside Australia, and I believe it was originated here by top Chinese restaurants because of the excellent quality of Australia's rock oysters, especially around the Sydney area. The salty flavor of the oysters blends superbly with that of the black beans, but the oyster must be the dominant flavor. This dish is a natural starter for a special dinner.

*12 very fresh oysters in
their shells
1 tbs chopped spring onions
or chives
2 tbs peanut oil
fresh coriander, ginger, red
capsicum and
parsley (to garnish)*

*for the sauce:
mix together
1 tbs black beans, mashed
slightly with the back of
a spoon
$\frac{1}{2}$ tsp sugar
$\frac{1}{2}$ tsp salt
dash of pepper
2 tsp chicken stock
$\frac{1}{4}$ tsp sesame oil*

serves 2

PREPARATION

Mix the black bean sauce ingredients together in a small bowl, and spoon a little on top of each oyster, together with the finely chopped spring onion (or chives).

TO COOK

Place the oysters in their shells into a steaming basket and steam gently for five or six minutes.

Just before the completed cooking time, heat the oil in a pot to smoking point, then pour a little oil over each oyster. The very hot oil is essential to give the final effect of flavor and texture. Garnish each oyster with a tiny sprig of fresh coriander and some finely chopped ginger and capsicum. Serve immediately.

Sesame Prawn Croutons

These delicious sesame prawn croutons are best eaten when hot, but they can be made earlier, then heated again in the oven for a few minutes.

6 slices stale white bread
  (toast bread is good)
3 tbs black sesame seeds
2 cups peanut oil

for the filling:
250g/8oz fresh shelled prawns
¼ cup water chestnuts,
  finely chopped
½ tsp salt
dash white pepper
1 tsp fresh ginger, finely minced
1 tsp egg white, lightly beaten
2 tsp corn flour

serves 2–4

PREPARATION

Cut round croutons using a scone cutter.

De-vein, wash, dry and chop the prawns to a rough mince consistency.

Mix together all the filling ingredients. Spread thickly onto the bread croutons, making a smooth mound in the centre. Make sure the prawn mixture is smoothed right to the edges.

Dip each crouton into the black sesame seeds.

TO COOK

Heat the oil in the wok until moderately hot. Slide in the croutons, mixture-side down. After approximately one minute, flip over to the other side and cook for another 30 seconds. Drain well, and serve.

fish Rolls

This is a modern version of a traditional Cantonese recipe in which the slices of fish are steamed with Chinese 'yunnan ham'. Yunnan ham is a famous ham in China, salty like prosciutto, but not available here in Australia. I wanted to serve this dish as a dim sum, and so I created this version.

*2 dried Chinese shiitake
    mushrooms, soaked 45
    minutes in warm water, then
    stalks removed and water
    squeezed out
4 spring onions
    (use mainly the white part)
400g/12oz sea perch
    or similar fish
salt and pepper to taste
4 wide ribbons of prosciutto
30g/1oz plain flour
½ egg white, lightly beaten
¼ cup fresh bread crumbs
2 cups peanut oil (for frying)*

serves 2

---

1 Place pieces of mushroom over each fillet, then one spring onion length on top.

2 Cover each piece with a ribbon of prosciutto then wrap it around the fish roll to secure the mushroom and spring onion, and press lightly to seal underneath.

PREPARATION

Slice the mushroom caps into julienne strips. Slice the spring onions into approximately 7.5 cm (3 inch) lengths.

Cut four even portions of fish approximately 5 cm x 4 cm (2½ inch x 2 inch) and sprinkle with salt and pepper. Place two to three pieces of mushroom over each fillet, then one spring onion length on top. Cover each piece with a ribbon of prosciutto then wrap it around the fish to secure the mushroom and spring onion, and press lightly to seal underneath.

Lightly coat the rolls with flour, brush with a little egg white and press evenly into the bread crumbs.

TO COOK

Deep-fry in moderately hot oil until crisp and golden. Drain and serve immediately.

1

2

Lamb and chicken satays on the charcoal brazier at Food Heaven Land, an outdoor cooked food market in Shanghai.

Singapore Noodles

Noodles are wonderful snack meals, good at any time of the day. They are satisfying and sustaining and, best of all, can be cooked in five minutes!

125g/4oz rice noodles (mai fun)
4 tbs peanut oil
½ tsp salt
60g/2oz onion, shredded
30g/1oz capsicum, shredded
2 tsp shredded ginger
30g/1oz fresh shrimps
4 dried Chinese shiitake
  mushrooms, soaked for 45
  minutes, stalks removed, then
  drained and shredded
30g/1oz char shui (Chinese roast
  pork — for convenience, buy
  it ready-cooked at Chinese
  stores or restaurants)
2 eggs, lightly beaten
2 tsp curry powder
1 tsp sambal oelek
1 tsp light soy sauce
small handful of bean sprouts,
  with untidy root ends removed
2 stalks spring onion, julienned

for the seasoning:
mix together
3 tbs chicken stock
¼ tsp salt
good pinch pepper

serves 2

PREPARATION

Place the noodles in a large bowl of hot water and stand for 15 minutes. Drain thoroughly and spread out to dry on a tray for at least 30 minutes. If desired, noodles can be prepared and refrigerated overnight.

TO COOK

Heat three tablespoons of the oil in a pre-heated wok until oil just begins to smoke. Add half a teaspoon of salt, then stir-fry the onions, capsicums, ginger, shrimps, mushrooms and char shui for a minute or two. Remove to a plate.

Add a little more oil to the wok, heat to a moderate temperature then add the beaten eggs to form a 'pancake'. When nearly set, add the noodles and fry over high heat, breaking the egg through the noodles. Stir in the curry powder, sambal oelek and light soy sauce.

Return the meat and vegetables to the wok and combine with the noodles. Stir in the spring onion and bean sprouts. Add the seasoning, mixing quickly and continuously over medium to high heat until the noodles are well-fried and golden.

Satays

Satays are substantial enough to stave off hunger pangs, are a natural for the barbecue, make delightful party food and can be presented as tasty entrées at any dinner party.

*250g/8oz rump steak, pork, lamb or
     chicken fillet (or some of each)*
250g/8oz fresh prawns, shelled
2–3 tbs peanut oil

for the marinade:
2 stalks lemongrass
2 tsp light soy sauce
*2 tsp shaohsing wine
     (Chinese rice wine)*
1 tsp sesame oil
good pinch salt and pepper
½ tsp sugar
1 clove garlic, minced
1 tsp ginger, minced
1 stalk spring onion
2 tsp corn flour
2 tsp Malay curry powder

for the satay sauce:
60g/2oz crunchy peanut butter
2 tsp peanut oil
2 tsp sugar
1 tsp sesame oil
1 tsp lemon juice
1 tbs light soy sauce
pinch salt and pepper
*⅓ tamarind block, soaked then
     squeezed and mixed with 2
     cups of warm water*

serves 2

PREPARATION

You will need bamboo satay sticks for this recipe. Soak them for at least two hours before you use them, otherwise they may burn when you grill or barbecue your satays.

To prepare your satays, cut the spring onion into 5 cm (approximately 2 inch) lengths. Mix together all the marinade ingredients in a bowl. Use only the tender inner section of the lemongrass and be sure to chop it very finely.

Cut the meat thinly across the grain into 5 cm x 2.5 cm (2 inch x 1 inch) pieces. Wash and de-vein the prawns. Place the meat into a bowl and mix well into the marinade and allow to stand for at least one hour.

Mix together the satay sauce ingredients in a bowl and put to one side.

Thread three or four pieces of meat onto each bamboo satay stick, laying the meat flat against the sticks. The prawns can be threaded on whole.

TO COOK

Grill under a normal domestic griller, turning once or twice, and marinating with a little peanut oil for about three or four minutes, until cooked. Serve with the satay sauce. Alternatively, the satays can also be grilled over an open charcoal fire.

Thai Chicken Salad with Green Mango

Thai salads are truly delightul. They refresh any jaded palate because of the tantalising and aromatic blend of fresh ingredients and spices.

4 pieces snow fungus, dried
1 chicken breast fillet, skinned
1 green mango
1 cup snow peas
¼ cup sesame seeds
2 tbs peanut oil
3 stalks spring onion, shredded
1½ cups fresh coriander,
    mostly leaves
1 clove garlic, finely chopped
¼ cup fried shallots

for the dressing:
mix together
¼ cup palm sugar, grated, then
    dissolved in a little hot water
    with a squeeze of lemon
1 tbs fresh lemongrass
    (use only the tender inner
    section and chop very finely)
½ cup lime juice
¼ cup fish sauce
2 fresh chilli peppers, seeds
    removed and finely chopped

serves 2

PREPARATION

Soak the snow fungus for 20 minutes. Rinse, squeeze out excess water and set aside.

Wash the chicken breast, pat dry with paper towels, and cut into finger-sized pieces and set aside. Peel and julienne the mango. Top and tail the snowpeas, blanch (plunge) in a pot of boiling water for one minute, and set aside.

TO COOK

Add the sesame seeds to a clean, dry wok, stirring them constantly over low heat until they turn a light golden color. Set aside as a garnish.

Add the oil to the wok and raise the heat. When the oil is just smoking, add the chicken pieces and stir-fry over moderate heat for one or two minutes until the chicken is cooked. Remove to a plate and allow to cool.

To assemble, combine the chicken and all the other ingredients, except the sesame seeds, spring onion and dressing, in a salad bowl. Slowly pour in the dressing, gently tossing the salad. Add the spring onion, sprinkle with the sesame seeds and serve.

Black Rice Pudding

Whenever I visit South East Asia I look for a place that serves black rice pudding, and I particularly like this version which I first discovered in Thailand.

Sticky black rice is a glutinous rice reserved for desserts, but it is only one of many rice varieties. On one visit to Vietnam, I was astonished to see a glorious array of colored rice displayed in large, crisp brown paper bags in markets — white, black, purple, green, yellow and even orange! The butterscotch sauce used in this recipe is my own addition to an otherwise traditional dessert.

250g/8oz sticky black rice (covered in cold water and soaked overnight)
90g/3oz crystallized ginger, finely chopped
60g/2oz glacé apricots, roughly chopped

for the butterscotch sauce:
100g/3½ oz butter
1 tbs golden syrup
1 tbs brown sugar
½ cup cream

serves 2–4

PREPARATION

Place the soaked and drained rice in a saucepan and cover with water to a height of three centimetres (black rice requires a little more water than white rice to cook). Cook using the absorption method (see Steamed Rice, page 22).

When the rice is cooked and whilst still at room temperature, combine with the ginger.

TO COOK

Gently melt the butter in a pan. Add the syrup and sugar until the sugar dissolves. Add the cream and stir until all is melted. Do not boil.

Spoon one tablespoon of the sauce into each serving dish. Top with the black rice mixture and serve garnished with the glacé apricots.

Promenading
on The Bund,
Shanghai.

'Traditional
Shanghai cuisine
consists of
seafood of every
description and
wonderful sweet
and sour
dishes.'

Shanghai Dumplings

These are a favorite in Shanghai and Beijing. The dough is rather heavier than that of the south, and the technique of frying first, then steaming in chicken broth, makes them a very substantial 'dot heart'. Serve with a dip of vinegar and shredded fresh ginger.

for the dough:
150g/1½ cups plain flour
1 cup hot water
2 tbs peanut oil
½ cup chicken stock

for the filling:
1 cup Chinese cabbage
*   (wong buk cabbage is best)*
220g/7oz topside steak, minced
30g/1oz fresh pork fat, chopped
*   to a mince (optional), or*
*   a little extra water*
2 tbs fresh coriander
1 tbs chives
1 tsp minced fresh ginger
¾ tsp salt
good pinch white pepper
2 tsp sugar
1 tsp light soy sauce
1 tbs corn flour

serves 2

PREPARATION

Blanch (plunge) the cabbage in a pot of boiling water just to soften. Drain well, then squeeze the water out by placing the cabbage between paper towels. Shred the cabbage finely.

Combine all the filling ingredients including the cabbage in a large bowl, and beat and knead until the mixture is soft and clingy. Chill in the refrigerator for about two hours.

Sift the plain flour into a stainless steel bowl. Make a well in the centre and add the hot water, gradually mixing at the same time with a wooden spoon until a fairly thick, soft dough is formed. Cover with a damp cloth and let stand for 20 minutes.

Remove the dough to a floured bench, and knead for another minute or two until the dough is smooth and pliable. Divide the mixture into two.

Roll each piece of dough into a sausage shape, approximately 2 cm (about ¾ inch) in diameter. Slice each 'sausage' at 2.5 cm (1 inch) intervals, to make approximately 10 pieces.

Press each piece into a circle with the palm of your hand, and roll into 8 cm (3 inch) rounds. Place 1½ teaspoons of filling into each round.

Close the edges together while pleating the side furthest away, then seal together (see step-by-step photographs on page 70). The dumpling is slightly curved because of the stretching of one side.

TO COOK

Heat the oil in a flat frying pan to moderate heat, and pan-fry the dumplings for two or three minutes, until the bottoms become crispy and lightly browned.

Add the stock to the pan. Continue to cook over moderate heat with a covered lid until the water has evaporated (about seven or eight minutes). Reduce heat to low, and continue to cook the dumplings for a further one or two minutes, to crisp up the bottoms again (add a dash of oil if necessary). Serve hot.

1 Roll each piece of dough into a sausage shape with a diameter of 2 cm (approximately ¾ inch). Slice each 'sausage' at 2.5 cm (1 inch) intervals, to make approximately 10 pieces.

2 Press each piece into a circle with the palm of your hand, and roll into 8 cm (3 inch) rounds. Place one and a half teaspoons of filling into each round.

3 Close the edges together while pleating the side furthest away, then seal together.

4 The dumpling is slightly curved. This is because of the stretching of one side.

1

2

3

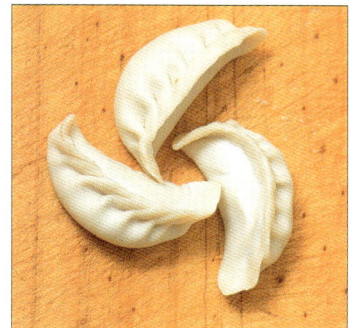

4

Wuxi Spareribs

The quantities set out for sparerib dishes are large, because they are good to put away for re-heating the next day.

½ kg/1lb pork spareribs in
*   bite-sized sections*

for the sauce:
mix together
¼ cup dark soy sauce
¼ cup sugar
½ tsp cloves
1 star anise
¼ tsp salt
small knob bruised ginger
1 stalk spring onion, chopped
*   (use mainly the white part)*
¼ cup water

to serve
steamed rice
few drops sesame oil
garnish of greens (parsley,
*   coriander, etc.)*

serves 2

TO COOK

Blanch (plunge) the ribs in boiling water for six minutes to remove excess fat and impurities. Remove and refresh under cold running water.

Simmer the sauce ingredients in a pot, add the ribs and simmer very gently for one hour, until the sauce thickens and is reduced to a coating consistency.

Just before serving, add a few drops of sesame oil. Serve with a garnish of greens and with steamed rice.

Sweet and Sour Salad

In Shanghai, traditionally the people like to have an array of appetisers before any important meal, and sweet and sour dishes are very popular. I first came across this dish in a journey back to the East some years ago and thought it offered an exciting alternative to the traditional vinaigrette salad dressings normally used in Australia at the time.

½ small continental cucumber
1 cup English cabbage
1 small green capsicum
½ bunch radishes
2 tbs peanut oil

for the sauce:
mix together
¼ tsp salt
1 tsp light soy sauce
¼ tsp sesame oil
1 tbs vinegar
1½ tbs sugar

serves 2

PREPARATION

Half-peel the cucumber, slice length-wise, remove seeds, and cut into finger-length strips.

Cut the cabbage into 2.5 cm (1 inch) squares.

Seed the capsicum and cut into 2.5 cm (1 inch) wedges. Top, tail and quarter the radishes, as you would an apple.

COOKING

Heat the oil until it is just beginning to smoke. Stir-fry the cucumber, radishes, cabbage and capsicum for two minutes.

Add the sauce, toss to combine well, then chill in the refrigerator before serving.

Grape Cluster Fish

This dish presents another skilful use of sweet and sour flavors. The key to it is the full-bodied chinkiang vinegar which gives quite a kick to the sauce. Served with the grapevine leaves — if you can find some growing nearby! — it is quite a talking point at dinner parties.

2 x 200g/13oz thick piece of
   white fish fillet with skin
1 tsp fresh ginger, grated
1 tbs spring onion, shredded
   (use mainly the white part)
1 tsp salt
1½ cups corn flour
grapevine leaves (or similar leaf)
   for a decorative garnish
2 cups peanut oil (for frying)

for the sauce:
mix together
1 tbs corn flour, dissolved in
   1 tbs cold water
3 tbs chicken stock
½ cup dark grape juice
¼ cup orange juice
1½ tbs chinkiang vinegar
2 tsp light soy sauce
1 tsp sugar
few drops peanut oil

serves 2

PREPARATION

Place the piece of fish, skin side facing down, on a cutting board and deeply score a criss-cross pattern diagonally across it, cutting down to the skin but not through it.

Place the fish in a dish and scatter with the ginger, spring onion and salt.

Stand for 15 minutes, remove ginger and spring onion, then coat thickly with corn flour.

Mix together the sauce ingredients.

COOKING

In a small wok or saucepan, boil the pre-mixed sauce ingredients for about three minutes, stirring constantly. Check the seasoning and keep the mixture warm.

Heat the oil in a large wok to smoking point, then reduce the heat slightly. Slide in the fish, skin side upwards, and deep-fry for about five minutes until golden brown and cooked through. As it cooks, the skin will curl up, giving the fish the appearance of a bunch of grapes.

Drain, place on a dish and arrange the vine leaves and stems at the top of the 'bunch'. (Do not eat the vine leaves or stems.)

Pour over the sauce and serve.

Early morning at West Lake, Hangzhou.
'Marco Polo said "Hangzhou is the finest and most splendid place on Earth".'

Drunken Chicken

As far back as the Han dynasty (202 BC-AD 220), wine has played an important role in Chinese culture and has helped to inspire the poets, painters and scholars of that land. In fact, the great Chinese poet, Li Po, is said to have drowned when inebriated while admiring the moon's reflection in the water. Whether or not this chicken dish will inspire new works of art is uncertain, but it is sure to elicit songs of praise in its honor.

It is also traditional for a Chinese husband to prepare drunken chicken (or wined chicken) for his wife after she has given birth, and to serve it to her along with words of affection and gratitude.

1 small roasting chicken
2 slices ginger
2 tsp salt
1 stalk spring onion, tied in a
  loose knot for easy removal
extra spring onion and ginger
  (for the garnish)

for the wine sauce:
mix together
2 cups shaohsing wine
  (Chinese rice wine)
1 tsp salt
¼ tsp sugar
1 tsp sesame oil

serves 2–4

TO COOK

Place the chicken, ginger, spring onion and salt in a pot and cover with water. Cover with a lid and bring to the boil, then simmer for ten minutes.

Turn off the heat and allow the chicken to stand in the stock until cooled. Chop the chicken into bite-sized pieces, arrange in a deep dish, then pour the wine sauce over it. It is traditional to retain the chicken bones, but you may remove them if you wish.

Marinate the chicken in the sauce overnight in the refrigerator. Turn the pieces occasionally.

Garnish with shredded spring onion and ginger, then serve.

Steamed Bean Curd with Fish Filling

Bean curd is such a valuable source of protein that it is sometimes called 'the cow of China' or 'poor man's meat'. Its flavor is quite bland, but because of the smooth spongy texture it absorbs and complements accompanying flavors beautifully. This light bean curd dish with a fish and dried shrimp filling is a natural choice for the diet-conscious, as it is high in nutrition and flavor and low in cholesterol and fats.

4 fresh bean curd squares
90g/3oz fish fillets
1 tsp har mai (dried shrimp)
½ tbs spring onions, finely
    chopped (use mainly the
    white part)
½ tbs fresh coriander, chopped
2 tbs corn flour (for dusting)

for the seasoning:
mix together
1 tsp light soy sauce
½ tsp sugar
½ tsp sesame oil
good pinch salt and pepper
2 tsp corn flour

for the garnish
2 tsp of sesame oil mixed
    with 2 tsp dark soy sauce
coriander sprigs

serves 2

PREPARATION

Soak the har mai for 30 minutes then chop finely.

Mince the fish fillet in a food processor or chop by hand, and blend until smooth. Add the dried shrimps, spring onions, coriander and seasoning.

Cut each bean curd square in half, and scoop out the centre to make a shallow well. Dust lightly with corn flour and shake off the excess. Stuff each bean curd square with the mixture, shaping the mixture smoothly into a mound in the centre.

TO COOK

Place the stuffed bean curds on a lightly oiled plate and steam gently over a low heat for five or six minutes.

Sprinkle each bean curd with the sesame oil and soy sauce and serve garnished with fresh coriander sprigs.

Note: The bean curd can be bought packaged in trays. Each tray can be cut into six or eight squares, each roughly 5 cm (2 inches) square.

Crispy Prawn Balls

There is a very definite art in deep-frying to achieve the correct results with these crispy prawn balls. Proper heat and timing are critical. The first minute of frying seals in the natural juices of the prawns and partially cooks the meat. The lowering of the heat at the next stage completes the cooking without toughening the fibres and drying out the meat, and the final quick burst of heat achieves the perfect color and crisp texture of the outside of the prawn balls.

250g/8oz fresh prawns, shelled, de-veined, washed and dried
1½ tbs pork (fatty pork is best)
4 water chestnuts, finely chopped
2 tsp corn flour
1 tsp egg white
salt
¼ tsp ground black pepper
½ tsp sesame oil
1 tsp shaohsing wine (Chinese rice wine)
1 tbs ginger, finely minced
1 tbs spring onions, finely chopped (use mainly the white part)
1½ cups white bread cut into tiny cubes
2 cups peanut oil (for frying)
Sichuan pepper and salt (prickly ash) for serving

serves 2

PREPARATION

These days you can buy ready-ground roasted sichuan pepper. However, to make your own 'prickly ash', mix together two parts salt with one part Sichuan peppercorns and roast in a hot dry pan for two minutes. Cool, then grind in a grinder (make-up a large quantity and use as needed).

To make your prawn balls, first chop the prawns and the pork to a mince and blend together into a smooth paste (either by hand or with a food processor). Place the mixture in a bowl and add the water chestnuts and corn flour. Mix together thoroughly. Gradually add the egg white, salt, pepper, sesame oil, shaohsing wine, ginger and spring onions. When well-combined, use your hands to pound the mixture against the side of the bowl to expel any air pockets (which could cause the prawn balls to break-up during cooking).

Shape into small balls about 2.5 cm (1 inch) in diameter and roll into the bread cubes to coat evenly.

TO COOK

Heat the oil in the wok until it is moderately hot then deep-fry the prawn balls a few at a time for about a minute (they should be a light color now). Lower the heat for 30 seconds, then turn the heat up to maximum for a final quick crisping for a further 30 seconds or so. Serve with the 'prickly ash' as a dip. Believe it or not, they're also great with tomato sauce.

Oyster and Prawn Spring Rolls

This is a luxurious version of the standard spring roll so loved in China and the rest of the world.

20 spring roll wrappers,
   each 125mm/5in square
2 cups peanut oil
1 tbs corn flour dissolved in a
   little water

for the filling:
½ cup bamboo shoots,
   finely diced
½ cup spring onions, chopped
   (use mainly the white part)
1 tsp ginger, finely minced
125g/4oz fresh shelled prawns
12 fresh oysters, shelled and
   roughly chopped
pinch salt and pepper to taste
1 tsp light soy

to serve:
sweet chilli sauce
squeeze of lemon or lime

serves 2

---

1 Spoon a portion of the mixture into each wrapper.
2 Lift the corner to completely encase the filling, then seal the edges with a little beaten egg. Fold in at the sides, and continue to roll to the end and seal, pressing firmly.

PREPARATION

Wash and de-vein the prawns, then chop roughly. Sprinkle the oysters with the salt and pepper, and fold together with the prawns. Add the bamboo shoots, spring onions and ginger then divide the mixture into 20 portions.

Spoon a portion of the mixture onto each wrapper, towards the middle and just down from the centre (see below). If you like, first strengthen the base of the spring roll by placing an extra half-wrapper on the lower section before spooning the filling on top. Lift the bottom corner of the wrapper to completely encase the filling, then seal the edges with a little of the corn flour and water. Fold in at the sides, and continue to roll to the end and seal, pressing firmly (work quickly so the juices of the oysters do not soak into the wrappers.)

TO COOK

Deep-fry in moderately hot oil for one or two minutes only, until light golden and crisp. Serve immediately with a dip of sweet chilli sauce and a squeeze of lemon or lime.

1

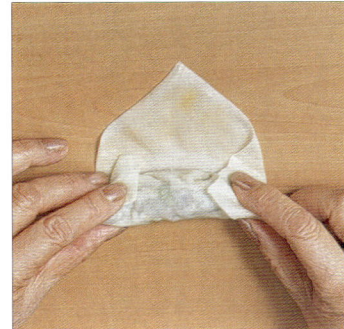

2

Hugong Temple,
Eighteen-Tea-Tree Royal Garden.

Tea bushes planted here a
thousand years ago still produce
tea today. In the 1840s, Emperor
Qianlong named the 18 trees
in front of the temple
'royal tea'.

Dragon Well Tea Prawns

An inspired dish from Hangzhou, combining two of Hangzhou's most celebrated ingredients, prawns and Dragon Well tea. Known as the 'Emperor's tea', Dragon Well tea is considered to be the finest in China. It owes its beautiful and unusual name to a Chinese legend which tells of two great dragons who live at the bottom of an ancient well in this region of China. It is said that when one stirs the waters of the well, the dragons can be seen below.

500g/1lb large fresh prawns,
　　shells removed and
　　tails intact
2 tsp Dragon Well tea leaves
2 cups peanut oil (for frying)
1 tsp ginger, finely minced
2 tbs chicken stock
1/2 tsp corn flour, mixed in 1 tbs
　　water (thickening)

for the egg white mixture:
mix together
1/2 egg white
1 tsp salt
1 tsp corn flour

serves 2

PREPARATION

Wash and de-vein the prawns, then pat dry using a clean towel. Place the prawns in a bowl containing the egg white mixture and mix well. Set aside.

Place the tea leaves in a cup and pour one cup of boiling water over the top. Allow to stand for ten minutes, then strain and discard the water.

TO COOK

Heat the oil in the wok until the oil just begins to smoke.

Deep fry the prawns until they change color to pink. Remove the prawns with a slotted spoon to a plate.

Drain off the oil from the wok, but leave a generous film of oil behind.

Sizzle the ginger briefly in the wok, then add the chicken stock. Stir in the corn flour thickening until smooth.

Return the prawns to the wok along with the tea leaves.

Toss together for a few seconds and serve immediately.

Sieu Mai

Here is the classic recipe for these little flowerpot dumplings. They are excellent for parties as you can steam so many at a time. Some won ton wrappers are quite small, but buy the larger wrappers for a perfect size. For beef sieu mai , ground topside beef may be substituted for the pork.

*30 won ton wrappers,
7.5cm (3in) square*

for the mince filling:
125g/4oz fresh shelled prawns
185g/6oz fresh fatty minced pork
½ cup water chestnuts
½ cup bamboo shoots
1 cup spring onion (use mainly the white part)
½ cup celery, finely diced

for the seasoning:
2 tsp salt
¼ tsp white pepper
2 tsp sugar
1 tsp fresh ginger, finely minced
1 tbs corn flour

for the dip:
*2 parts soy sauce mixed with
1 part sesame oil*

serves 2–15

1 Hold the wrapper and place some filling in its centre.

2 Wrap the sides up and around, squeezing the wrapper close to the filling so the top gathers into pleats. Pack firmly.

PREPARATION

Wash and de-vein the prawns and chop to a mince. Combine with the pork. Finely chop the water chestnuts, bamboo shoots, spring onion and celery. Mix the filling ingredients together in a bowl, then add the combined seasoning ingredients. Knead until smooth then chill for at least 30 minutes.

Hold a wrapper in your palm and place a tablespoon of filling in its centre. Wrap the sides up and around, squeezing the wrapper close to the filling so the top gathers into pleats. Gently push the filling down from the top to pack the 'flowerpot' firmly, and top up with extra filling if needed. The filling should be seen above the wrapper.

TO COOK

Flatten the bases slightly and place over boiling water in a lightly oiled bamboo basket or on a lightly oiled plate, and steam for 15–20 minutes. Serve with the dip.

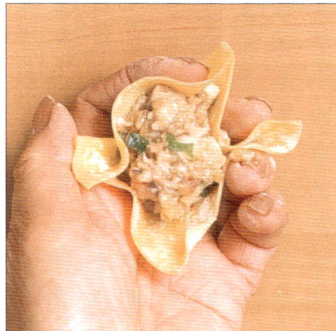

1

2

Steamed Spareribs in Black Bean Sauce

Pork spareribs, apart from being an economical way to enjoy China's favorite meat, is enjoyed for its highly flavorsome quality, particularly when it is teamed with a robust sauce made from the salted black soya bean.

This is a family dish found commonly in rural southern China. It is interesting to see the inclusion and the popularity of this homestyle dish in the yum cha menus of today.

2 tbs peanut oil

2 tbs black beans,
    rinsed under cold water,
    drained and chopped roughly

¼ tsp salt

2 cloves garlic, chopped

1 tsp sugar

2 tbs chicken stock

2 tsp shaohsing wine
    (Chinese rice wine)

2 tbs light soy sauce

1lb/500g pork spareribs,
    chopped through in bite-sized
    sections between the ribs

1 tbs corn flour

2 red chilli peppers,
    chopped

2 tbs fresh coriander, chopped

serves 2

TO COOK

Heat the peanut oil in a hot wok, and sauté the black beans gently with salt, sugar and garlic for ten seconds before adding the chicken stock, the wine and the light soy sauce.

Simmer together for 30 seconds. Remove the sauce to a mixing bowl, and blend in the spareribs and allow to marinate for at least 30 minutes.

Add the corn flour, mixing well through the spareribs, then place the ribs on a plate ready for steaming.

Sprinkle over the red chilli peppers and the chopped coriander, and steam over boiling water in a bamboo steamer for 45 minutes.

Paper-Wrapped Fish

This method of rolling meat or fish up with seasonings and other ingredients is typical of the Chinese love of small parcels and little tasty dishes. The cooking of the dish in this way creates a concentration of flavors inside the little 'mystery package'. When the package is opened, the tantalising aromas and flavors are released.

1 large sheet of baking paper or Chinese rice paper
2 tbs sesame oil
4 good spinach leaves, washed and dried thoroughly
squeeze of lemon juice
185g/6oz filleted fish, boned and skinned (ocean trout or sea perch)
salt and pepper (to taste)
¼ cup bamboo shoots, shredded
½ cup fresh shiitake mushrooms
3 tsp spring onions, white part only, shredded
1 tsp ginger, minced
1 egg, lightly beaten

serves 2

PREPARATION

Cut four 15 cm (6 inch) circles from the paper, and generously brush each circle with oil, using a pastry brush.

Trim the spinach leaves to fit neatly over the paper circles.

Cut the fish into four 5 cm (2½ inch) squares.

Top each spinach leaf with a piece of fish and sprinkle with salt and pepper. Squeeze a little lemon over the top. Arrange a little bamboo shoot, mushroom, spring onion and minced ginger over each piece of fish.

Roll the spinach leaf firmly around the fish and the other ingredients to completely wrap into a little parcel.

Brush the edges of the baking paper circles with a little beaten egg, and wrap over the spinach and fish roll, folding in the edges like a parcel. Brush the tops with the remaining egg.

TO COOK

Place in the oven to cook at 200°C (410°F) for about five minutes. Serve in the paper and unwrap to reveal the fragrant flavors and juices at the table.

Note: Chinese rice paper, which is edible, can be used instead of the baking paper. It is available from most Asian foodstores.

The skyline at dawn, near the
Forbidden City, Beijing.

Peking Duck Roll

A contemporary version of the wonderful Chinese dish, Peking Duck. It is heartier than the more traditional version and, served as a sliced roll rather than in the usual delicate manner, it makes an excellent snack.

4 spring roll wrappers,
    25cm/10in square
8 tbs hoi sin sauce
4 lettuce leaves (mignonette or
    butter lettuce)
2 cups carrot, shredded
2 cups cooked roast duck,
    shredded
2 cups continental cucumber,
    unpeeled and coarsely
    shredded
extra hoi sin sauce (for serving)

serves 4

PREPARATION

Place one spring roll wrapper diagonally on a bench (so it is shaped like a diamond). Brush the entire wrapper with two tablespoons of hoi sin sauce.

Place one lettuce leaf on top of the wrapper, then spread half a cup of shredded carrot in a roll shape across the lettuce leaf, just down from the centre (see step-by-step photographs on page 102).

Top the carrot roll with half a cup of shredded duck, followed by some shredded cucumber. Fold the corner of the wrapper over to completely enclose and wrap the filling. Fold in the sides and tightly roll up, shaping as firmly as possible to form a nicely rounded roll. Moisten the edges if necessary with a little hoi sin sauce. Repeat with the remaining ingredients to make a total of four rolls.

TO SERVE

Slice each roll diagonally into three equal portions and serve with hoi sin sauce.

1 Place one spring roll wrapper diagonally on a bench. Brush the entire wrapper with two tablespoons of hoi sin sauce. Place one lettuce leaf on top, then spread the shredded carrot in a roll shape over the lettuce. Top the carrot roll with half a cup of shredded duck, followed by half a cup of cucumber.

2 Fold the corner over to completely enclose and wrap the filling.

3 Fold in the sides of the wrapper and roll it up firmly.

4 Continue rolling, shaping as firmly as possible as you go to form a nicely rounded roll.

1

2

3

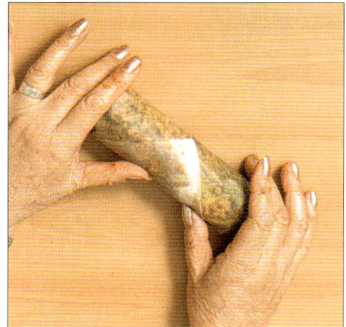

4

Facing page:

Elizabeth at the tea house, Dragon Well tea plantation.

'The finest tea in China comes from the Dragon Well tea plantation, near Hangzhou. Producing a beautiful light liquor, the green tea produced here is unfermented and has served the courts of emperors for centuries.'

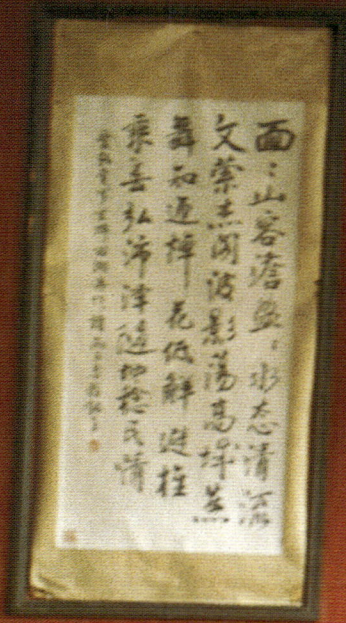

Cellophane Noodle Salad

This recipe is extremely simple to prepare and is most refreshing on a summer's day. The colors and textures are very interesting all the way through — slippery noodles, crispy carrots, cucumbers, apples and nuts, all mixed together in a tangy fresh sauce. It also looks very pretty!

60g/2oz cellophane (sometimes
    called 'glass' or 'transparent')
    noodles (fun si)
90g/3oz carrots, julienned
1 continental cucumber,
    unpeeled and julienned
1 small apple, julienned (skin on)
1 small pear, julienned (skin on)
60g/2oz Chinese sweet pickles,
    julienned
30g/1oz peanuts, with
    skins on

for the dressing:
mix together
2 tbs sesame oil
2 tsp vinegar
$^1/_2$ tsp salt
1 tsp sugar

serves 2

PREPARATION

Place the peanuts on a tray and toast in a moderately hot oven for 10–15 minutes.

Soak the noodles in warm water until soft (about 20 minutes). Drain and cut into approximately 10 cm (4 inch) lengths.

Combine the noodles with the carrots, cucumber, apple, pear, pickles and peanuts in a bowl. Chill in the refrigerator.

Arrange on a serving plate. Add the dressing to the vegetables.

Silky Tofu and Thousand Year Old Eggs

Thousand year old eggs (also called 'century' or 'dynasty' eggs) are preserved duck eggs and are extremely rich in flavor.

The eggs are first placed in a mixture of ash and earth, then put in a dark, cool receptacle. Preservation occurs over 10–12 weeks. Their unusual, rich and exotic flavor blends well with the silky tofu used in this recipe. Japanese silky tofu, which is sometimes mixed with egg and has a silkier texture than usual tofu, can be purchased in a roll (which I prefer) or cake form from most super-markets or Chinese food stores.

2 x 150g rolls Japanese
   silky tofu
2 1000-year-old eggs
3 stalks spring onions (use
   mainly the white part)
3 tbs fresh ginger juice or
   ginger, finely minced
1 cup pine nuts, finely chopped
3 tbs peanut oil
1 tsp salt

serves 5

PREPARATION

Cut each silky tofu roll into ten equal slices. Remove the outer casings from the eggs, rinse briefly, then roughly chop.

Finely chop the spring onion, then mix with the ginger in a bowl and put aside.

Dry roast the pine nuts in a dry pan over low heat for a minute or two, until lightly toasted (don't burn them). When roasted, finely chop the pine nuts and place in a separate bowl.

TO COOK

Heat the peanut oil with the salt in a small pot until it is just smoking, then pour it over the spring onion and ginger mixture in the bowl. Add the chopped eggs.

PRESENTATION

To make a base for this dish, spread the finely chopped pine nuts over a round serving plate. Arrange the 20 tofu slices, beginning in a circle at the perimeter of the plate. Place approximately one teaspoon of the chopped egg mixture onto each tofu slice, then serve.

Braised Fish
in Soy Chilli Sauce

A hot, spicy dish, it is at its best when served with steamed rice and perhaps a quick stir-fried green vegetable, such as beans, broccoli or Chinese cabbage.

1 flathead or garfish, or other fish
    fillets weighing approximately
    250g/8oz
3 tbs peanut oil

for the sauce:
mix together
1 small clove garlic, minced
1 tsp soy chilli sauce
2 tsp light soy sauce
¼ tsp sugar
3 tbs water
½ tbs spring onion, chopped
pinch of salt

for the thickening
½ tsp corn flour, mixed with
    1 tsp water

for the garnish:
extra spring onion, chopped

serves 2

PREPARATION

Wash and scale the fish well. Pat dry with a paper towel.

TO COOK

Heat the oil to smoking point in a wok or frying pan and fry the fish for two or three minutes on both sides. Remove with a slotted spoon.

Drain off excess oil from the wok, leaving about one tablespoon behind. Add the sauce ingredients, mix well, then simmer together for a minute or two before returning the fish to the wok. Simmer uncovered for another three minutes, then remove the fish to a serving plate.

Thicken the sauce with the corn flour thickening, then pour the sauce over the fish and serve sprinkled with spring onions.

farmers herding

ducks to market.

'To talk about

Beijing food is

to talk about Peking

Duck, the legendary

dish which has

carved its way into

immortality the

world over.'

Quick Stir-fried Noodles

This quicky, tasty meal can be prepared in minutes. Fresh noodles need only to be dunked in boiling water, drained and left 'floating' in warm water until needed.

60g/2oz chicken or beef
2 rounds of Chinese dried egg noodles (or equivalent in fresh)
a handful of bean sprouts, tailed
½ bunch garlic chives, chopped into 5cm/2½ in lengths
2 tbs peanut oil

for the marinade:
mix together
½ tsp light soy sauce
½ tsp sesame oil
1 tsp shaohsing wine (Chinese rice wine)
½ tsp corn flour

for the seasoning:
mix together
1 tsp light soy sauce
2 tsp min si jeung (ground bean sauce)
1 tsp soy chilli sauce
¼ tsp salt
¼ tsp sugar
2 tbs chicken broth (preferably), or water

serves 2

TO COOK

Slice the meat into thin slices and place in the marinade for about 20 minutes (strips of meat should not be marinated for lengthy periods).

Add the noodles to a pot of rapidly boiling water, until just cooked (soft, but slightly chewy). Most fine Chinese noodles only need one minute on the boil. Drain and quickly add a few drops of oil to keep the noodles from sticking together.

Heat the remaining oil in the wok and stir-fry the meat over high heat until the color changes.

Add the garlic chives, and cook for a further 30 seconds. Combine the noodles thoroughly in the wok with the meat. Add the bean sprouts, then stir in the seasoning and combine thoroughly.

Eggplant Shells

The eggplant's pithy interior makes it ideal for stuffing. Its exotic flavor and texture lends itself to quite strong companions such as black bean.

300g/10oz small eggplants,
250g/80z fresh shelled prawns
2 fresh bean curd squares
*   (see note on page 83)*
a little egg white
extra corn flour for dusting
3 cups peanut oil (for frying)

for the seasoning:
1 tsp salt
good pinch white pepper
1 tsp shaohsing wine
*   (Chinese rice wine)*
½ egg white, lightly beaten
1 tsp corn flour

for the sauce:
½ small onion, finely chopped
2 tsp salted black beans,
*   drained and mashed with the*
*   back of a spoon*
1 clove garlic, finely minced
1 tbs red capsicum, finely diced
2 tsp light soy sauce
1 tsp oyster sauce
salt and pepper (to taste)
1 tsp sugar
½ cup chicken stock
2 tsp corn flour mixed in a little
*   cold water (thickening)*

serves 2

PREPARATION

Slice the eggplants across their width at 1 cm (approximately ½ inch) intervals. Cut through on each alternate slice to make open eggplant shells.

Wash and de-vein the prawns and dry on a paper towel, then chop finely. Coarsely chop the bean curd, then combine the prawn and bean curd very thoroughly to make a smooth paste. Add the seasoning and mix thoroughly.

Fill each eggplant shell with the prawn and bean curd mixture between the slices, to make sandwiches. Smooth the edges to neaten. Brush the tops with egg white, and dust each lightly in corn flour.

To make the sauce, gently sauté the onion in two tablespoons of peanut oil, until softened. Add the black bean and garlic to the onion. Stir in the remaining sauce ingredients except the thickening. Bring to a gentle boil, stir in the thickening for a few seconds, then set the sauce to one side.

TO COOK

Heat the wok and add the remaining peanut oil. Heat until moderately hot. Fry the eggplant shells until they are lightly crisp and golden on one side, then turn and fry on the other side for a further three minutes.

Drain on a paper towel, then serve topped with the sauce.

Mandarin Beef

The full-bodied spicy sauce used in this dish is characteristic of the food of north China where the climate is very cold. The northern people shred their meat rather than slice it, as they do in the south. Prepared in this way, it cooks very quickly and forms part of the rich sauce. It goes well with the bread buns found in north China.

250g/8oz eye fillet,
   cut in thin strips
½ white onion, sliced
1 small green capsicum,
   julienned
2 spring onions, shredded
2 cups peanut oil (for frying)

for the marinade:
mix together
½ egg, lightly beaten
1 tsp corn flour
1 tsp sesame oil
1 tsp peanut oil

for the sauce:
mix together
2 tsp dark soy sauce
3 tsp chinkiang vinegar
½ tsp salt
¼ tsp pepper
1 tbs tomato sauce
3 tsp worcestershire sauce
2 tsp sugar
1 tsp peanut oil

serves 2

TO COOK

Add the beef strips to the marinade then deep-fry the beef strips in the peanut oil until golden brown. Remove the beef with a slotted spoon and drain the oil from the wok, leaving about one tablespoon of oil behind.

Add the onion and capsicum and stir-fry briefly before returning the beef to the wok. Toss together for one minute.

Add the sauce to the wok and continue to simmer on a moderate heat for a further one or two minutes. Add the spring onions and serve.

Chinese Roast Duck Salad

This is another way to enjoy Beijing's famous ducks. It is most often served as a small dish to herald a banquet in China, but elsewhere in the world it simply makes a delightful little salad.

1 cup carrot, julienned
1 cup continental cucumber, julienned
½ Chinese loh buk (white radish), julienned
2 tsp salt
½ Chinese roast duck and duck sauce (available at Chinese take-away restaurants)
4 tbs vinegar
4 tbs sugar

for the garnish:
2 tbs sesame seeds
fresh coriander, several sprigs
2 stalks spring onion, shredded

serves 2

PREPARATION

Place the carrot, cucumber and loh buk in a mixing bowl. Sprinkle salt over the top of the julienned vegetables and let stand for 30 minutes, then drain off all the resultant liquid.

De-bone the duck, then slice off all the skin leaving a thin layer of meat still attached to it. Julienne the skin very finely. The remaining meat is not required for this recipe and can be used to make another duck-inspired dish.

TO COOK

Using a small pot, add the vinegar and sugar and boil to dissolve the sugar. Remove from heat and allow to cool. Pour this mixture over the vegetables, mix through thoroughly, then refrigerate.

Place the sesame seeds into a dry fry pan, heat and stir slowly until the seeds turn a golden brown color. Put aside as part of the garnish.

Combine the julienned duck with the refrigerated vinegared vegetables. Add two tablespoons of the duck sauce and mix through to flavor the salad.

Garnish with a sprinkling of sesame seeds, coriander and spring onion. Serve without delay.

A selection of local chillies and spices at the street market in Chengdu, Sichuan Province. 'Sichuan is the Texas of China; everything here is bigger, heartier, stronger and gutsier than anywhere else . . .'

Shoulder Pole-carrying Noodles

I was introduced to this delightful noodle dish in Chengdu, capital city of the Sichuan province, while strolling through its city streets. The fragrant aroma of Sichuan's wild peppercorns reached me and, fascinated, I watched a young man serving steaming noodles in bowls, topped with a tasty-looking meat sauce. He had bowls, chopsticks and all his ingredients in two bamboo baskets which were strung at both ends of a bamboo pole. It was mid-winter, and business was brisk. After the rush was over, he simply picked up the bamboo pole, balanced it deftly across his shoulders and moved his 'restaurant' to another street.

I hurried back to my hotel to inquire more of this marvellous snack, and learned it has always been a familiar sight in Sichuan. My friendly chef prepared it for me and I have been cooking it ever since — without, however, taking it out into Australian streets on a bamboo shoulder pole!

250g/8oz fine noodles
2 tsp sesame oil
2 tbs peanut oil
250g/8oz topside beef,
*   finely minced*
pinch Sichuan peppercorns
1 tbs chopped spring onions
½ tsp soy chilli sauce
2 tsp red vinegar
2 tsp soy sauce
2 tbs chicken broth
extra spring onions or coriander

for the seasoning:
2 tsp light soy sauce
½ tsp salt
1 tsp sugar
1 tbs shaohsing wine
*   (Chinese rice wine)*

serves 2

COOKING

If you are using fresh noodles, cover them with hot water and allow to stand for three minutes. Drain and rinse briefly.

If using packaged noodles, drop the noodles into a pot of boiling water and stir to separate. When the water comes to the boil, add one cup of cold water and cook until the water boils again. Drain the noodles in a colander and rinse briefly under cold water.

Place the cooked noodles in a bowl and mix in the sesame oil. Keep warm over a pot of hot water.

Heat the oil in a pre-heated wok and stir-fry the meat mince until the color changes (about one or two minutes). Add the seasoning ingredients, and combine well.

Place the Sichuan peppercorns in a hot wok (no oil) and stir over a low heat for a few minutes until they are dark brown and fragrant. To crush, grind in a coffee grinder or blender. (Make up a large quantity and use as required.)

TO SERVE

Using two bowls, place in each bowl: one teaspoon of chopped spring onion, a quarter of a teaspoon of the soy chilli sauce, one teaspoon of vinegar, one teaspoon of soy sauce, a good pinch of crushed Sichuan peppercorns and one tablespoon of chicken broth.

Cover with a large handful of noodles, top with meat, then garnish with chopped spring onions or a sprig of coriander. Just before eating stir the noodles in the bowls to mix with the seasonings.

Facing page:

A Muslim boy creates a piping hot, fragrant noodle dish in minutes at a street stall.

Smoked Rainbow Trout

You will want to keep some of this in the refrigerator for those many times when you want a special snack! Those of us who live alone develop some rather unusual times for eating, and there seem to be many occasions when it is just too late for cooking, but just right for a light, tasty meal of a few cracker biscuits, some cheese, and this beautiful smoked trout. Hence the larger-than-usual recipe. The process of smoking meats in China is primarily for flavor rather than for cooking.

2 fresh rainbow trout
2½ cups peanut oil (for frying)
1 tbs Chinese Oolong or
    Jasmine black tea
1 tbs sugar

for the marinade:
mix together
2 tbs minced ginger
3 tbs shaohsing wine
    (Chinese rice wine)
3 tbs dark soy sauce
2 tbs chopped spring onions
2 tsp sugar
2 tsp salt
¼ tsp white pepper

serves 2–4

PREPARATION

Wash and dry the fish well.

Place the fish into the marinade and allow to stand for two hours. Turn the fish occasionally.

TO COOK

Heat the oil in the wok until just smoking.

Gently slide in the fish and deep-fry for five minutes. If the oil doesn't quite cover the fish, occasionally spoon the hot oil over the fish while it cooks. When cooked, remove the fish and drain on a paper towel.

Wipe out the wok and place the tea leaves and sugar into the bottom of the wok. Sprinkle with water. Cover with the lid, and turn on to a low heat. When the tea leaves begin to smoke, place the fish on a wire steaming rack in the wok. Cover with the lid and smoke for 15 minutes over a low heat then serve.

Note: For this recipe, I like to line the wok with foil before I smoke the tea leaves. This helps to protect my wok, and when the fish is smoking (with the lid on the wok), the foil helps to keep all the smoke inside it.

Sichuan Dry-Fried Snake Beans

The technique of dry-frying is unique to Sichuan cuisine. The method (often called 'explosion cooking') involves first frying the ingredients, then finishing by placing them in a hot dry wok. When the fried ingredients hit the hot dry wok the effect is like a small explosion.

Snake beans are so called because they are long, soft, and tend to curl around in coils. They are also called 'yard beans'. They are generally readily available at Chinese greengrocers, but if not French beans may be substituted with equally flavorsome results. Use snake beans if you can, as the visual appeal is quite spectacular.

250g/8oz Chinese snake beans
2 cups peanut oil (for frying)
1 clove of garlic, chopped
½ tsp ginger, finely chopped
½ tsp salt
1 fresh red chilli pepper, finely
    chopped
1 tsp sugar
1 tsp light soy sauce
4 tbs water
½ tsp sesame oil

for the garnish:
1 tbs red capsicum, finely diced
1 tbs brazil nuts, finely diced
1 stalk spring onion, chopped

serves 2–4

PREPARATION

Top and tail the snake beans, and break into 12 cm (5 inch) lengths (but if using French beans, leave them whole).

TO COOK

Heat sufficient oil in the wok for deep-frying the beans. Raise the temperature until the oil begins to smoke, then reduce to a moderate heat.

Carefully lower the beans into the oil and deep-fry for about four minutes until they are softened and appear slightly wrinkled. Remove with a slotted spoon, drain and set aside.

Pour off the oil, allowing approximately one tablespoon to remain in the wok. Heat the wok until the oil begins to smoke, then briefly sauté the garlic, ginger, salt and chilli over a moderate heat. Return the beans and combine with the other vegetables in the wok.

Add the sugar, the soy sauce and approximately four tablespoons of water and, maintaining moderate heat, stir-fry until the resultant sauce is reduced and the beans are almost dry. Add the sesame oil, toss well and transfer to a serving plate. Garnish with the diced spring onions, capsicum and nuts then serve.

Ma Po Bean Curd

A hot and spicy dish from Sichuan, with smooth, creamy bean curd complemented by an unusual hot yet piquant sauce. The Sichuan wild pepper (fagara) is responsible for this sensation and is grown only in that province. Take care when frying it for the first time. It can be deceptively mild at first, then after a moment or two it takes effect and a general numbing sensation spreads through the mouth. It is hot in a different way to most pepper . . . and the distinct fragrance is as much a part of the ingredient as the flavor.

½ tsp Sichuan pepper
2 tbs peanut oil
125g/4oz pork, minced
4 bean curd squares
   (see note on page 83)

for sauce A:
2 tsp light soy sauce
2 tsp soy chilli sauce
1 red chilli pepper, diced
1 tsp garlic, finely minced
1 tsp ginger, finely minced

for sauce B:
½ cup chicken stock
2 tsp shaohsing wine
   (Chinese rice wine)
pinch salt
1 tsp corn flour dissolved
   in a little water
½ tsp sugar

for the garnish:
2 tbs spring onions, chopped

serves 2–4

PREPARATION

Dry roast the Sichuan pepper in a hot dry pan until lightly cooked then grind to a powder (see page 123 for more detailed instructions).

Mix together the ingredients for the two sauces in separate bowls.

TO COOK

Heat about two tablespoons of oil in a hot wok, and when smoking stir-fry the pork until the color changes.

Add sauce A, stirring until the sauce comes to the boil, then stir in the bean curds. Gently combine in sauce B, tossing through the bean curds.

Serve with the Sichuan pepper and the spring onions sprinkled on top.

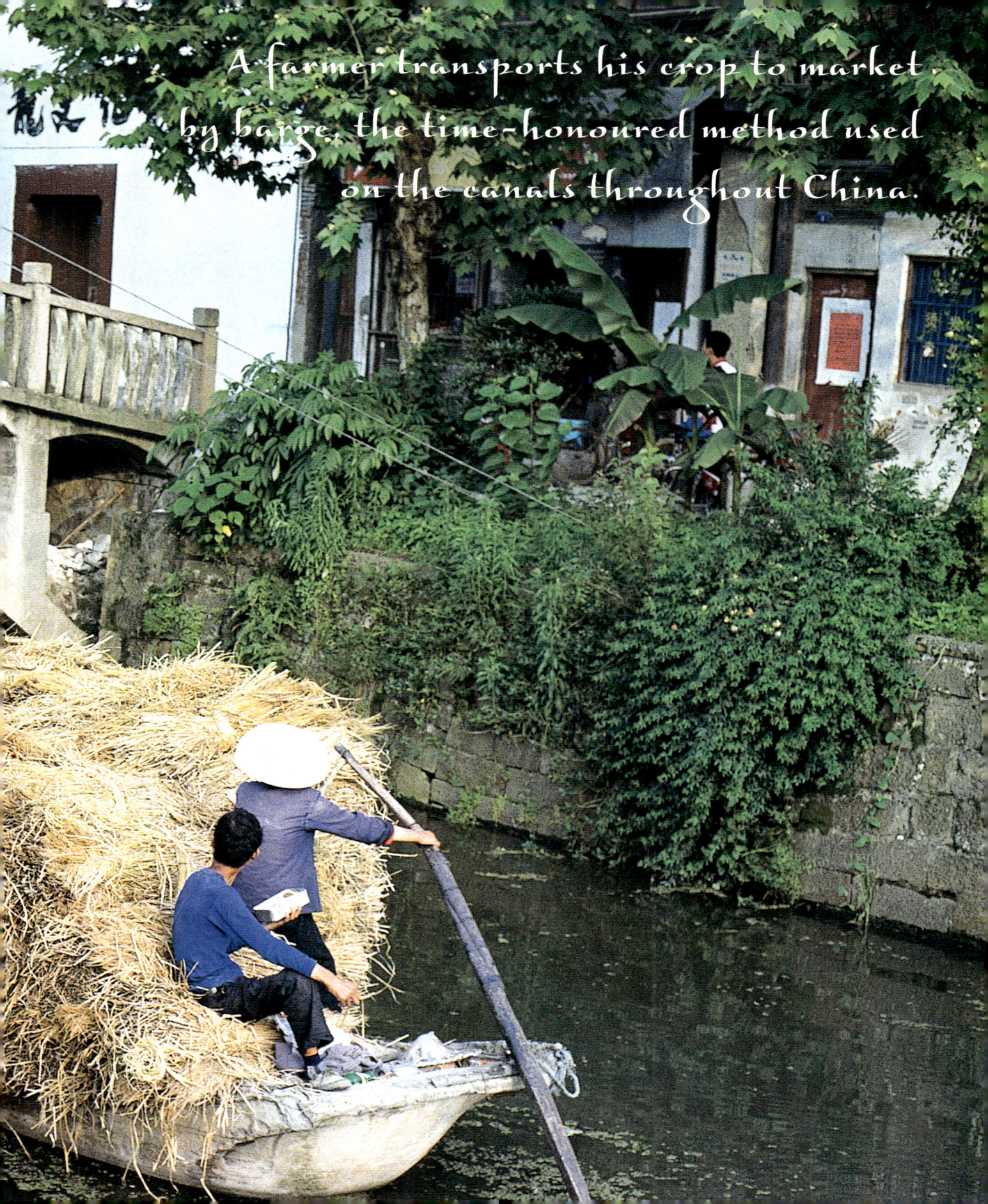

A farmer transports his crop to market
by barge, the time-honoured method used
on the canals throughout China.

Sichuan Sour Hot Soup

This is Sichuan's famous soup. It is heartier in flavor than Cantonese soups and features the Sichuan peppercorn, fagara, which is a native of Sichuan province and is present in a number of their dishes. When combined with their fiery hot chilli peppers, the effect is quite numbing, literally!

¹/₄ tsp Sichuan pepper
2 tsp chinkiang vinegar
2 tsp light soy sauce
2 tsp chopped spring onion
¹/₂ tsp chillies, chopped
1 tsp ginger, minced
1 tsp coriander, cut into
    2.5cm/1in lengths)
90g/3oz pork meat, sliced thinly
1 tbs peanut oil
4 cups water or stock
¹/₄ tsp salt
¹/₂ tsp sugar
¹/₄ cup bamboo shoots, julienned
¹/₂ tbs cloud ear fungus
2 tsp corn flour dissolved in
    a little water
2 fresh bean curd squares,
    cut into 1cm/¹/₂ in julienne
    strips (see note on page 83)
1 egg, lightly beaten

for the marinade:
¹/₂ tsp light soy sauce
few drops sesame oil
1 tsp corn flour
¹/₂ tsp sugar

serves 2

PREPARATION

Dry roast the Sichuan pepper in a hot, dry pan until lightly toasted. Grind to a powder (see page 123 for more detailed instructions).

Mix together the marinade ingredients. Marinate the pork strips briefly. Separately, soak the cloud ear fungus in water for 30 minutes, then drain and rinse.

Place the vinegar, soy sauce, spring onion, Sichuan pepper, chillies, ginger and coriander into a serving soup tureen. Put to one side.

TO COOK

Stir-fry the pork slices over a medium heat in the peanut oil in a soup saucepan until the pork changes color.

Add the water (or stock) to the saucepan, together with the salt and sugar. Bring to the boil, then add the bamboo shoots and cloud ear fungus. Simmer for five minutes.

Mix in the corn flour and water mixture and stir until the soup is boiling and is of a velvety consistency. Add the bean curd, then gently stir in the beaten egg until the egg floats in soft tendrils.

Immediately pour over the ingredients in your serving tureen and serve.

Spicy Eggplant

This is one of my favorite dishes. I like to serve it at dinner parties at my home, and my guests always love it. It is a simple and quick dish to prepare and, served with hot steamed rice, it makes a satisfying meal in itself. Eggplant is a popular vegetable in China, and has a long history. It is said that the society ladies of Ancient China also used the skin of the eggplant as a cosmetic. It stained their teeth dark, which was considered attractive.

2 small eggplants
1 tbs peanut oil
60g/2oz pork, minced
2 tsp ginger, minced
2 cloves garlic, minced
1 stalk spring onion, chopped
    (use mainly the white part)
1 tsp soy chilli bean sauce
1 tsp corn flour dissolved in a
    little water

for the seasoning:
mix together
¼ cup chicken stock
1 tbs light soy sauce
pinch of salt
pinch of pepper
½ tsp sugar

serves 2

PREPARATION

Top and tail the eggplants. Slice each eggplant in half and then into thick finger-length strips.

TO COOK

Heat the oil in a pre-heated wok and bring to smoking point. Stir-fry the minced pork until the color changes, then add the minced ginger, garlic and spring onion and stir-fry until fragrant.

Add the soy chilli sauce, mix through, then add the eggplant to the meat mixture.

Toss quickly over high heat before adding the seasoning. Simmer for two minutes, then add the corn flour and water mixture, stirring gently until the sauce takes on a silky texture. Serve hot with steamed rice.

Sesame Beef Balls in a Spicy Sweet and Sour Sauce

A great dim sum or entrée and also makes an excellent hor d'oeuvre when served with drinks. Place a toothpick in each one before serving.

500g/1lb topside or rump steak,
    finely ground
1 clove garlic, minced
1 tsp ginger, minced
¼ tsp pepper
1 tbs light soy sauce
a little egg
1 tbs corn flour
2 tbs sesame seeds,
    lightly toasted
2 cups peanut oil (for frying)

for the sauce:
mix together
1 tbs vinegar
1 tbs sugar
1 tbs tomato sauce
½ tsp chilli sauce or
    sambal oelek

serves 4

PREPARATION

Mix the mince and all the ingredients except for the oil, sesame seeds and sauce mixture together thoroughly. Pound the mince mixture into the sides of the mixing bowl several times, as this will make the meat hold together (otherwise, they will crack during deep-frying).

Divide the beef mixture and make-up 20 meatballs.

Put the sesame seeds into a dry wok and stir them constantly over a low heat until they turn a light golden color. Remove them and put to one side.

TO COOK

Heat the oil to about 200°C (400° F), adding about six balls at a time to cook. Deep-fry until they are golden brown. Remove and drain.

Drain off the oil from wok, wipe with a paper towel then pour the sauce mixture into the wok. Stir over low heat for a few seconds, then add the cooked meatballs to the sauce. Stir well for one minute so the sauce covers the meatballs. Stir in the sesame seeds so they coat the meatballs, then transfer the meatballs to a serving plate and serve.

Note: For a sweeter variation of this dish, add two teaspoons of fresh orange zest and a tablespoon of orange juice to the sauce.

Chairman Mao's Little Red Fish

Chairman Mao's addiction to hot spicy foods during his long march is well documented, and I named this dish in his honor. I have a copy of his Little Red Book *and now I have his Little Red Fish, so my collection is complete!*

300g/10oz white fish fillets such as red emperor, rockling or sea perch
pinch salt and pepper
a dusting of corn flour
2 tbs peanut oil
3 slices ginger
2 cloves garlic, peeled and sliced
1 red chilli pepper, chopped
1 stalk spring onion cut into 5cm/2in lengths (use mainly the white part)

for the spicy sauce:
mix together
2 tsp ground bean sauce
2 tsp sweet chilli sauce
1 tbs shaohsing wine (Chinese rice wine)
½ tsp sugar
1 tbs chinkiang vinegar
3 tbs chicken stock

for the garnish:
finely shredded red capsicum and spring onions

serves 2

PREPARATION

Mix together the spicy sauce ingredients and put to one side. Next, salt and pepper the fish fillets, and dust with a little corn flour.

TO COOK

Heat the peanut oil in the wok until it begins to smoke. Add the ginger slices then add the fish fillets and fry over a moderate heat for four minutes on each side. Remove to a plate and discard the ginger.

Drain off the oil, reserving one tablespoon. Wipe out the wok and return the reserved oil to the wok. Add the garlic, chilli pepper and spring onions and sizzle until there is a release of fragrance.

Stir in the spicy sauce and simmer for one or two minutes to release the flavors. Return the fish to the wok to braise in the sauce for three or four minutes, turning the fish as it cooks.

Serve immediately, garnished with spring onions and red capsicum shreds.

'The Wan Chai street markets are the fresh produce mecca for rich and poor alike. Everybody shops here.'

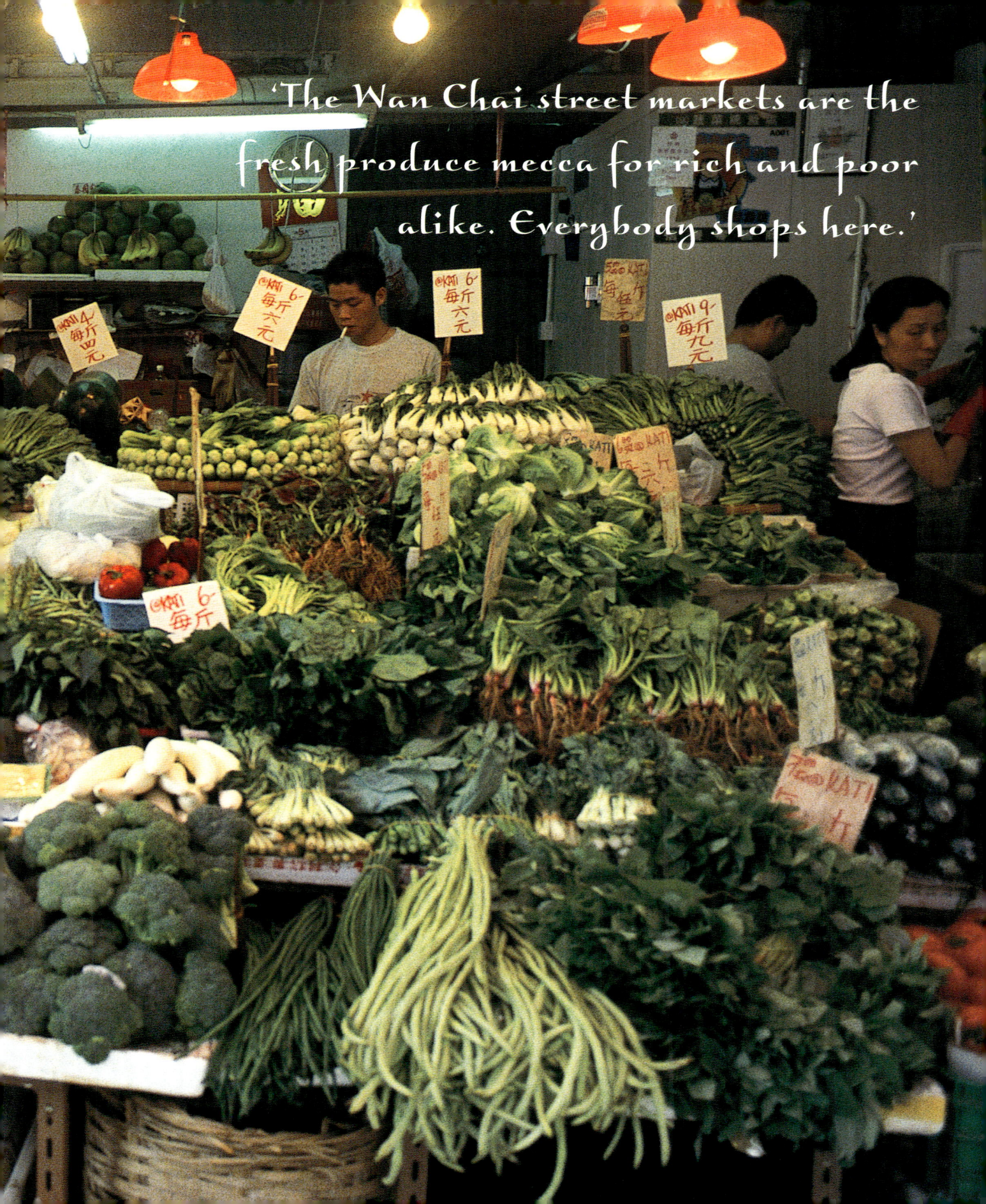

Steamed Beef Balls

These beef balls are extremely light and smooth — you will enjoy them!

small piece of dried
   mandarin peel
250g/8oz finely minced beef
1 tsp salt
1 tsp sugar
1 tsp corn flour
1 spring onion, chopped (use
   mainly the white part)
1 tsp sesame paste
dash of pepper
1 tsp light soy
1 tbs peanut oil

serves 2

PREPARATION

Soak the mandarin peel in warm water until soft and chop finely. Put to one side.

Combine the beef, salt and sugar with three tablespoons of hot water and mix thoroughly. Marinate the beef for 30 minutes.

Put the beef into a mixing bowl and pound against the sides of the bowl. (This dispels air pockets and ensures that the meatballs will not crack during cooking.)

Add the corn flour to the mince whilst still pounding. Mix well with the mandarin peel, spring onions, sesame paste, pepper and soy sauce. Finally, add the oil, a little at a time, and continue to pound the meat mixture until it is blended thoroughly.

TO COOK

Fashion the meat mixture into small meatballs, about the size of ping pong balls. Arrange in the steamer and steam for eight to ten minutes.

Crystal Prawns

This is a classic Cantonese dish. It is simple and elegant, but the success of the dish relies entirely upon the delicate appearance of the crystal prawns.

8 fresh shelled prawns, with
    tails intact
20 snow peas, topped and tailed
2 cups clear chicken stock
2 cups peanut oil (for frying)
1 tsp garlic, finely chopped
1 tsp ginger, finely chopped
¼ tsp red chilli pepper,
    finely chopped
2 tsp corn flour (for dusting)

for the prawn marinade:
½ tsp salt
½ tsp white pepper
1 tsp egg white,
    lightly beaten
1 tsp corn flour

for the thickening:
½ tsp corn flour mixed in 2 tsp
    cold stock or water

serves 2

PREPARATION

First wash and de-vein the prawns. Place the prawns in a large bowl of cold water with the water running. Rinse and 'beat' the prawns through the running water for about 10 minutes; this will give them the 'crystal' look. Drain and dry well and place in the refrigerator for at least one hour.

Work the marinade into the prawns and return to the refrigerator.

Blanch (plunge) the snow peas in the two cups of boiling chicken stock for 30 seconds, then remove and drain. Reserve three tablespoons of the stock for the sauce.

Blanch the prawns in the peanut oil for 10 seconds, then remove and drain. Leave two tablespoons of oil in the wok.

TO COOK

Add the garlic, ginger, and chilli pepper to the heated wok and stir quickly for about 15 seconds. Add the reserved stock, then stir in the thickening to make a velvety sauce.

Return the prawns to the wok, and toss quickly over a high heat together with the spices and snow peas.

Chicken and Crabmeat Pies

These pies are great favorites in Hong Kong's yum cha restaurants. The traditional Chinese pastry is very sweet but I prefer to use short pastry which has a light crumbly texture. The filling is absolutely delicious, and if you can get fresh crab meat do so, as the flavor will be even better.

2 tbs peanut oil
185g/6oz minced chicken
2 tbs chopped spring onions
¼ cup water chestnuts,
    finely chopped
¼ cup bamboo shoots,
    finely chopped
90g/3oz crab meat,
    drained and flaked with a fork
500g/1lb ready-rolled
    short pastry
a little beaten egg for glazing

for the seasoning:
mix together
2 tsp corn flour mixed with
    2 tbs water
1 tbs shaohsing wine
    (Chinese rice wine)
1 tsp sesame oil
½ tsp salt
¼ tsp pepper
½ tsp fresh ginger, minced

serves 4–6

PREPARATION

Heat the peanut oil in a pre-heated wok until it is just smoking. (This is called 'the breath of the wok'.) Stir-fry the chicken mince until the color just begins to change, then add the spring onions, water chestnuts, bamboo shoots and crab meat.

Toss together over high heat for a minute, then make a well in the centre and stir in the seasoning. Continue to stir until the mixture thickens. Remove to a plate, and allow to cool completely.

Using an 8 cm (3 inch) scone cutter, cut out approximately 20 pastry rounds from the ready-rolled pastry, to make about ten pies.

Pre-heat the oven to 200°C (400°F). When the meat mixture is cold, place about two teaspoons into each pastry round, and cover with another round. Press edges to seal, then pleat together to make a plaited finish. Brush with a little beaten egg to glaze.

COOKING

Place the little pies on an ungreased tray and bake for 15 minutes. Alternatively, they can be deep-fried in moderately hot oil for 5 minutes.

Lobster in Ginger Sauce

This dish is enjoyed in China on special festive occasions such as Chinese New Year. I like to use lobster tails, which are more economical and have much less waste than full lobsters (a large part of which is shell and is hence discarded). Plan this dish for a special dinner for two; it is served with the ruby red shell still in place, giving it a very festive appearance.

1 lobster tail

3 cups peanut oil (for frying)

1/4 cup fresh ginger, cut in thick
   slices and bruised with the
   back of a chopper

1/2 cup spring onions cut in
   5cm/2in lengths (use mainly
   the white part)

good pinch salt

pinch pepper

1/2 tsp sugar

2 tsp shaohsing wine
   (Chinese rice wine)

1/2 tsp light soy sauce

1/2 cup chicken stock

for the marinade:

mix together

1 tbs egg white

1/4 tsp salt

dash of white pepper

1 tbs corn flour

for the thickening:

1 tsp corn flour mixed in a
   little cold water or stock

serves 2

PREPARATION

Chop the lobster tail through the shell into good bite-sized pieces. Work the marinade mixture into the lobster and let it stand for about five minutes.

TO COOK

Heat the peanut oil in a hot wok until the oil is smoking, then reduce to a moderate heat. Add the lobster pieces to blanch in the hot oil for one minute. Remove the lobster with a slotted spoon, drain and put to one side. Drain and reserve the oil from the wok, and wipe the wok clean.

Return two tablespoons of the reserved oil to the wok, heat to smoking point, and sizzle the ginger and spring onions for 30 seconds. Return the lobster to the wok and stir-fry over a high heat for another few seconds. Add the salt, pepper, sugar, soy and wine and continue to stir-fry quickly. Add the chicken stock, cover with the wok lid, and cook for one minute.

Stir in the corn flour thickening until the lobster pieces are glazed. Serve immediately.

'Hong Kong, a city that can't or won't stand still. It lives in the present and is one of the most exciting and vibrant places on Earth.'

Salmon Fillets
with Black Bean Dressing

A contemporary Chinese dish. Unlike traditional Chinese dishes, I feel this dish works best when served on individual plates. With the lovely pink salmon highlighted with the lush black bean dressing, and served with a fresh garden salad, this is the best of the East and the West.

4 fresh salmon pieces
¼ tsp salt
¼ tsp pepper
shaohsing rice wine
   (Chinese rice wine)
2 tbs olive oil

for the black bean dressing:
1½ tbs black beans
1 fresh small red chilli pepper
2 cloves garlic
2 slices ginger
½ tsp sugar
¼ cup light soy sauce
1 tbs olive oil
¼ cup light chicken stock

for the garnish:
½ cup spring onion, shredded
1 cup chopped coriander
   (use mainly the leaves)
1 small red chilli pepper, washed
   and sliced finely

serves 2

PREPARATION

Salt and pepper the salmon, then splash a little shaohsing wine over the fillets and allow to stand while you make the dressing.

To prepare the dressing, place the black beans in a bowl, rinse in a small amount of cold water, then drain off the water. Using the back of a spoon, squash the beans (apply only light force and avoid mashing them into a paste).

Slice the red chillies lengthwise, remove the seeds and slice finely. Add the chillies, garlic and ginger to the black beans. Also add the sugar, light soy sauce and one tablespoon of the olive oil. Put to one side.

TO COOK

Heat two tablespoons of the olive oil in a non-stick frying pan over moderate heat. Slide in the salmon skin-side down and pan-fry for one or two minutes. Turn and cook for a further three or four minutes on the other side, until tender. Remove to a plate, and keep warm. Sauté the black bean mixture in the same frying pan over moderate heat for one or two minutes. Now add the light chicken stock and allow to simmer for a further minute. Place a salmon fillet on each serving plate, spoon on some of the black bean dressing and garnish with spring onion, coriander and a few slices of chilli.

Rice Noodles with Three Kinds of Mushrooms

This dish can be cooked at a moment's notice. It is a welcome recipe for vegetarians, and mushrooms are a natural companion for the noodles. It is wonderful now to be able to buy such a wide range of exotic mushrooms at supermarkets, so make good use of them. I also particularly like the slippery texture of the rice noodle ribbons used in the dish.

*375g/12oz ho fun noodles
(fresh rice noodles)*
3 tbs peanut oil
*6 fresh shiitake mushrooms,
sliced*
½ cup fresh oyster mushrooms
½ cup fresh enoki mushrooms
*200g/7oz snow peas, cut into
fine julienne strips*
*¾ cup spring onions, shredded
(for the garnish)*

for the seasoning:
mix together
1 tsp light soy sauce
1 tbs oyster sauce
good pinch salt
good pinch pepper
½ cup chicken stock
1 tsp sesame oil
pinch sugar

serves 2

PREPARATION

Ho fun noodles are often sold in a square block. For this recipe, simply cut the block into 1.25 cm (½ inch) wide ribbons before cooking.

TO COOK

Heat the peanut oil in a pre-heated wok and stir-fry all the mushrooms together with the snow peas for one minute.

Stir in the seasoning, then mix the noodles thoroughly in the wok taking care not to break them as they soften while cooking.

Finally, toss through the shredded spring onion and serve.

Spicy Chilli Squid

The Chinese have a fondness for seafood, and squid is a great favorite. However, as a child I remember if I asked my mother to do some typically time-consuming thing, she would respond: 'So! You must think I've got time to cook squid!' This must be the Chinese equivalent to 'So you think I've got time to watch the grass grow'. No doubt it refers to the time-consuming preparation of squid, but thankfully we can now buy the clean tubes ready for cooking.

300g/10 oz fresh squid
    (calamari) tubes
2 tbs corn flour (for dusting)
½ red chilli pepper, diced finely
1 small clove garlic,
    finely chopped
½ cup red capsicum,
    cut into 2cm/1in dice
½ cup green capsicum,
    cut into 2cm/1in dice
2½ cups peanut oil (for frying)

for the spicy salt:
2 tbs sea salt
¾ tsp five spice powder
freshly ground black pepper

serves 2

PREPARATION

To make the spicy salt, heat a clean dry pan or wok until very hot. Add the salt, reduce the heat and roast on a gentle heat for three or four minutes until the salt becomes fragrant. Stir in the five spice powder and black pepper.

Using a sharp knife, open each squid tube down the centre lengthwise, and open out flat. Wash under cold running water, removing the membranes. Place on a cutting board with the inside facing up and score with shallow diagonal criss-cross cuts at 5 mm (¼ inch) intervals. Cut each piece into 5 cm (2 inch) wide triangular pieces. Dry well on paper towels, then dust very lightly with the corn flour. Shake off any excess and put aside on a plate with the vegetables.

COOKING

Heat the oil to a moderate heat in the wok and deep-fry the squid for about one minute. It will curl and take on a light golden hue and will be 70% cooked. Remove it with a slotted spoon, then drain the oil from the wok leaving about one tablespoon behind.

Briefly sauté the garlic, capsicums and chilli pepper. Add the squid and toss quickly over a high heat for a couple of minutes, sprinkling with spicy salt as you go. Finally, turn the heat up to maximum for the last 30 seconds. This removes any excess oil and gives a lovely dry finish.

Ginger Cream

This is a modern adaptation of an old favorite served at big banquets called almond jelly. Both are enjoyed at the closure of a big dinner. This dish cleanses the palate and provides a perfect finish to a big Chinese meal because it is so clean and refreshing.

5 tsp gelatin, dissolved in 3 cups of hot water
3 tbs sweetened condensed milk
½ cup crystallized ginger, finely sliced

for the syrup:
90g/3oz Chinese slab brown sugar or rock sugar
½ cup water

to serve:
extra slices of crystallized ginger

serves 2–4

PREPARATION

When the gelatin mixture has cooled, stir in the condensed milk. Add the crystallized ginger. Pour into small individual sweet dishes, and set in the refrigerator for two hours.

TO COOK

Bring the sugar and the half cup of water to the boil in a small saucepan. Simmer for about five minutes until slightly thickened. Allow to cool, then chill in the refrigerator for about one hour.

Arrange some extra slices of the crystallized ginger on top of each ginger cream. Spoon one tablespoon of syrup over each, then serve.

GLOSSARY

Chinese cuisine incorporates a wide range and ever-increasing array of ingredients. The glossary below provides the names and brief descriptions of the more unusual ingredients used in this book, but is not intended to be comprehensive. The recipes in *Tiny Delights* have been carefully prepared to include authentic but readily available ingredients. Most can now be purchased at good supermarkets and Chinese food stores and if not substitutes are provided. Where ready-made ingredients are purchased (such as noodles, wrappers, tinned and jarred vegetables and the like), follow the manufacturer's instructions on the packaging for preparation and storage advice.

bamboo shoots
The shoots of the bamboo tree, available fresh or canned. The fresh bamboo shoots are covered with a thick layer of leaves which are removed before using. Canned bean shoots will keep for several weeks in the refrigerator after opening; cover with cold water and change the water daily.

bean curd
This is made from soy beans and is a rich source of protein, so much so that it is often called in China 'poor man's meat'. The soy bean itself is sometimes called 'the cow of China'. Soft, fresh bean curd has a texture similar to custard, and is sometimes added to soups or deep-fried as a companion to other ingredients.

bean paste, hot
This hot and slightly salty paste is made from soya beans, chillies and oil.

bean sprouts
The shoots of the soya bean or the mung bean (the soya bean sprouts are much larger). Fresh bean sprouts will keep for several days if refrigerated.

black beans
These lightly salted beans are fermented black soya beans. They have a strong, pungent flavor and are generally crushed and used with fish or beef.

brown bean sauce
see *min si jeung*

buk choy
Chinese white cabbage, with a dark green leaf and a white crisp stalk. It is used in stir-frying.

cabbage, Chinese white
see *buk choy*

cabbage, tientsin
see *wong buk choy*

char shui
Chinese sweet roast pork.

chilli paste
A condiment produced from ground chillies, garlic and other spices.

chilli pepper
A small, very hot vegetable used frequently in Chinese cooking. It needs to be chopped finely before use. The seeds add extra heat and can be removed if preferred.

Chinese roast pork
see *char shui*

Chinese sausage
see *lup chiang*

Chinese white radish
see *loh buk*

cilantro
see *coriander*

cloud ear fungus
This dark brown fungus has a bland taste, musky aroma and a crunchy texture.

coriander
A leafy green herb with a highly aromatic, almost sweet, flavor. Also known as 'cilantro'.

corn flour
A finely-ground maize flour used as a thickening agent; it produces clear, velvety sauces. Also known as 'corn starch'.

corn starch
see corn flour

doong choi
Salted and preserved Chinese vegetable (often cabbage or turnip). It adds a savoury flavour to some meat dishes (particularly minced meat) and soups.

dried shrimp
see *har mai*

fagara
The wild peppercorn, also known as 'Sichuan pepper' or 'brown peppercorns'. If not ready-ground, the peppercorns should be dry-roasted before use then ground. This pepper has a pungent flavor and aroma.

fish sauce
Made from dried fish, this thin light-brown sauce is used as a seasoning or condiment.

five spices powder
A fine blend of Sichuan pepper (*fagara*), cinnamon bark, clove, fennel and star anise (or aniseed).

flying fish roe
fish eggs, including caviar.

fried shallots
These can be purchased at most Chinese food stores.

garlic
Almost as important as ginger, fresh garlic is used for many dishes, especially for beef. Use only fresh garlic.

ginger, crystallized
sweet preserved ginger (usually dried and sugared).

ginger, fresh root
The fresh ginger root is a vital ingredient in Chinese cooking. It freshens meats, especially seafoods and poultry, and imparts an indefinable sharp sweetness to cooking oil and soups. Old ginger root has thick, rough skin and possesses a strong flavor suitable for soups and slow-cooked meat dishes. Tough skin may be carefully removed, but do not cut too deeply as much of the flavor lies directly under the skin.

glutinous rice
see sticky rice

ground bean sauce
Like *min si jeung* (brown bean sauce), this is a pungent salty sauce made from soya beans but in this version the beans are finely ground to make a smoother sauce.

ground nut oil
see peanut oil

har mai
Very small dried shrimps, quite strong in flavor, and often used to flavor dumplings.

hoi sin sauce
A sweet and tangy seasoning sauce produced from red beans, soya beans, sugar and spices.

lemongrass
A grass with a bulb-like base, and which has a distinctive lemon flavor. The outer layers should be removed and only the tender inner section at the base used for cooking. If slices of lemongrass are used as a flavoring, they should be discarded before serving the dish. If the lemongrass is to remain in the dish, it should be very finely chopped otherwise it is inedible.

loh buk
This is a Chinese turnip. It looks like an overgrown white carrot. It has a strong flavor and smell, but is very good in soups and some stir-fried dishes. It can also be grated to make savoury tidbits.

lup chiang
A tasty, sweet pork sausage smoked and faintly redolent of Chinese rice wine. They hang in pairs suspended by hooks in every Chinese grocery store and are popular in home cooking. They are placed to steam over the rice when it has almost completed its steaming stage.

mandarin peel, dried
More specifically called tangerine peel in China. They are pieces of sun-dried mandarin peel and are quite expensive to buy. They give a unique flavor to certain stewing and duck dishes.

min si jeung
A pungent, salty sauce which is made from soya beans and is very important in some meat dishes where it gives a characteristic color as well as flavor. It is also used for roasting duckling and is often an important marinade for barbecuing pork. It is surprisingly good with potatoes.

mushrooms, dried
These are dried shiitake mushrooms and are beloved by the Chinese and are used in a great variety of ways. They are graded for size and thickness and although

they are quite expensive, the Chinese home always has a supply. They are soaked for approximately 45 minutes in warm water in which time they will become spongy and bouncy and return to their original size. They can be used, sliced or whole, as a valuable ingredient in many dishes.

mushrooms, fresh

A wide variety of fresh mushrooms are available at supermarkets and greengrocers today. These include:
straw: these are a little like French champignons and have a delicate taste and an intriguing shape. They are used as a 'contrast' ingredient in a dish, providing interest.
shiitake: fresh shiitake mushrooms have an earthy, smoky flavor, and are not as strong as the dried version.
oyster: these mushrooms have a delicate flavour and exotic appearance.
enoki: a Japanese mushroom with a delicate flavor.

noodles

A wide range of noodles is used in Chinese cuisine. Most types can be purchased fresh or dried, and require little preparation. They are produced from either rice, wheat flour, or occasionally mung bean flour.

nori sheets

Traditionally used in Japanese sushi, these are flat, dried seaweed sheets. They are used in Chinese cooking, often in soups.

oyster sauce

A thick dark brown fermented sauce produced from oysters and soy sauce. Although made from oysters, it does not possess a 'fishy' taste.

pandanus leaves

These large leaves are used as a flavoring in cooking and sometimes as a wrap. Once the dish is cooked and the flavour imparted, the leaf is discarded.

peanut oil

Oil made from peanuts often used for deep or shallow frying, and also to blend other ingredients. Also known as 'groundnut oil'.

prawns

These crustaceans should always be purchased fresh or fresh frozen. Look for flesh that is firm and slightly blue-grey in color. They are usually shelled, washed, dried and de-veined before cooking (to de-vein, remove the black gritty thread along the back before cooking), although for some dishes they are served in their shells.

preserved vegetables

An infinite range of preserved vegetables are used in Chinese cooking. Preserving methods include salting, sun-drying, and pickling. Also see *doong choi*.

prickly ash

a mixture of salt and ground Sichuan pepper (*fagara*). It is sprinkled on dishes, and also sometimes used like a condiment.

rice

For the southern Chinese, rice is life. There are three main varieties: long grain, short grain and glutinous. Long grain and short grain rice grows profusely in China and are staples in the Chinese diet. Glutinous rice, which is a short grain variety, is richer and heavier and sometimes called 'sweet rice'. When cooked it turns almost transparent and very sticky. It is used mainly in sweets and desserts. Black glutinous rice is also available.

rice paper

Used as a wrap in cooking, this is an edible paper produced from the pith of a tree.

sambal oelek

Malaysian hot chilli sauce.

sausage, preserved

see *lup chiang*

sesame oil

Used in very small quantities as a flavoring, this is an aromatic oil produced from sesame seeds and has a slightly nutty flavor. It is never used for cooking.

sesame paste

Also known as 'tahini', this is a creamy paste made from ground sesame seeds and sometimes blended with oil.

sesame seeds

The small seeds of the sesame plant. White sesame seeds are used in sweets and fillings and for making sesame paste. The black sesame seeds are used to make a thick sweet soup of distinctive flavor. Both types of seed are occasionally used to form a coating over another food, and also as a garnish.

shaohsing wine

Chinese rice wine from Shaohsing.

shrimps

These small crustaceans should be purchased fresh

or fresh frozen. They usually require minimal preparation; just rinse thoroughly before adding to your cooking. They should not be used as a substitute for *har mai* (dried prawns) which is a special Chinese ingredient.

Sichuan peppercorns
See *fagara*

snake beans
Also known as yard beans, these have a softer, meatier texture than French beans. They are very long and tend to curl and coil around themselves, hence their name.

snow peas
Crisp green pea pods, eaten whole. They should be topped and tailed before use.

soy chilli sauce
Used extensively in Chinese cooking, in spicy dishes. Made from soya beans and chilli, it has a full texture.

soy sauce
Sauces extracted from the soya bean. Light soy sauce is thinner in substance and has a lighter flavor and color than dark (or 'mushroom') soy.

spring roll wrapper
Paper-thin wrappers made from soft flour and water and dried into a white, skin-like wrapper. They are usually purchased frozen, in packs of 25 or 50, and should not be exposed to the air for too long as they will crack and become unusable.

squid
Also known as 'calamari', this small mollusc resembles a cuttlefish.

star anise
A star-shaped spice with eight points. It is sold in 'points' (broken), whole or ground and has a strong anise flavor.

sugar, slab
A sugar produced from dark-brown semi-refined sugar.

sugar, rock
A crystallized sugar, also known as rock candy.

tabasco sauce
A spicy Western sauce made from chilli peppers which has found its way into Chinese cuisine.

tamarind
This seed grows in a large pod, but is usually purchased as a processed block. It is sometimes necessary to soak in warm water before adding to dishes.

thousand year old eggs
Preserved duck eggs, sometimes called 'dynasty' or 'century' eggs.

tofu, silky
A rich, silky bean curd, sometimes blended with other ingredients such as egg. It is usually purchased in tubes or tubs.

turnip, Chinese
see *loh buk*

vinegar, chingkiang
A deep brown, strongly flavored vinegar made from glutinous rice.

vinegar, red
A bright, amber-colored rice vinegar, used as a condiment for seafood dishes and also for flavoring sauces.

water chestnuts
The bulb-like stem of the tule or other bulrush. They are crisp in texture and sweet in flavor. Canned water chestnuts will keep for about a month after opening, if covered with fresh water and refrigerated (change the water daily).

wong buk choy
A pale green cabbage, tightly packed like young celery. Delicately sweet in flavor and used in soups and stir-fry dishes.

won ton wrappers
These wrappers are made from high-gluten flour and eggs. They are used to wrap a variety of dim sum dishes. The wrapper can be purchased fresh or frozen, in small and large sizes.

yunnan ham
A famous ham produced through salting and smoking. Substitute fine quality ham or prosciutto.

zest
finely-grated citrus peel (orange, lemon or lime).

ACKNOWLEDGEMENTS

The complex process of producing a television series and its companion book require the creativity, support and courage of many people. In particular I would like to thank Emma Borghesi, John Hay, James Tan, Caroline Velik, Valeriu Campan and John Leonard for their creativity, Miryana Power, Gerry van den Broek, Nigel Roberts, Sam Cheah, Samantha Bragg and Helen Wong for their support, and Mark Henry, Andrew Cronin, Stephen Cheung, MaryAnn Ellis, Yvonne Grant, Paul Ritchie, Sam Cutera, Paul Tozer and Leigh Jeffs for their courage. And I must sincerely thank Elizabeth Chong, without whose talent and patience none of this would have been possible. Thank you all.

The Sponsors whose logos and contact details appear below did more than just commit time, money and their products and services to this project, they also believed in the dream. Please support them.

—— Ron Brown
Producer and Publisher

BROWN BROTHERS MILAWA VINEYARD

Milawa, Victoria
www.brown-brothers.com.au

SMEG APPLIANCES

Hagemeyer Australia
www.hagemeyer.com.au

HO MAI CHINESE APPERTISERS

Makmur Enterprises
www.makmur.com.au

KIKKOMAN SAUCES

www.kikkoman.com.au

ORIENT EXPRESS ANTIQUES

Melbourne, Australia
tel: +61-3-9421 3288

LA IONICA POULTRY

www.laionica.com.au

FURI KNIVES

www.furitechnics.com.au

FISSLER COOKWARE

Cambur Industries
toll free (Australia only): 1800 337 313
www.cambur.com.au

BUDERIM GINGER

www.buderimginger.com

GRANDVIEW KITCHENS

Melbourne, Australia
tel: +61-3-9729 8211

GALLERY INDOCHINE

Melbourne, Australia
tel: +61-3-9815 0068

HELEN WONG'S TOURS

www.helenwongstours.com

HONGKONG TOURISM BOARD

www.discoverhongkong.com

王府飯店
THE PALACE HOTEL
Beijing

花园酒店
The Garden Hotel
GUANGZHOU

Great Eagle Hotel
HONG KONG
鹰君酒店

AUTHOR'S ACKNOWLEDGEMENTS

My first word of appreciation goes to Ron Brown, producer of my current television series, *Elizabeth Chong's Tiny Delights,* who, in the making of the film, created the vehicle for this companion book to the series, and inspired me to pick up my writing pen again.

The team assembled to bring this project to fruition includes some wonderful hard-working and immensely creative professionals.

Thank you Emma Borghesi, designer and editor of *Tiny Delights: the companion to the TV series*, who smoothed all the rough edges in her expert and gentle way, making my work more a joy than a chore.

John Hay, photographer, who with Caroline Velik, food stylist, combined their outstanding artistry and talents to capture the true spirit of 'tiny delights'. The photographs are simply beautiful, and readers will surely delight in this book because of them.

My appreciation also to Orient Express of Melbourne, for their lovely Chinese and Asian artefacts and antiques, which lent so much character and elegance to my food.

And of course my heartfelt thanks to friend and colleague, James Tan, who was invaluable to me both personally and professionally. With his unique talent and flair, he was my pillar of strength in the kitchen.

I am indebted to this great team of true professionals who made this wonderful project possible.

—— Elizabeth Chong